American Corporate Identity 97

The 12th Annual showing the best new work in the U.S.A.

David E. Carter

Editor

Suzanna M.W. Brown
Book Design

Library of Congress Catalog Card Number:

ISBN: 0-688-15056

FCI Publishing Co.
2843 Brownsboro Road
Louisville, Kentucky 40206

Phone: 502-896-9644
Fax: 502-896-9594

For sales in the USA and Canada:

Watson-Guptill Publications
1515 Broadway
New York, NY 10036

Phone: 800-451-1741
   * in NJ, AK, HI call 908-363-4511
Fax: 908-363-0338

For sales outside the USA and Canada:

Hearst Books International
1350 Avenue of the Americas
New York, NY 10003

Phone: 212-261-6770
Fax 212-261-6795

Jacket design by Bill Butler

Printed in Hong Kong by Everbest Printing Company,
through Four Colour Imports, Louisville Kentucky.

Table of Contents

Complete
Identity Programs

Client: **IBM**
Design Firm: **Lippincott & Margulies**
Designers: **Connie Birdsall, Rodney Abbot**

7

Client: **Radio Shack**
Design Firm: **Landor Associates**
Designers: **Jeff Pascoe, Judy Hemming,
Nat Plummanus Caesarchin, Scott Drummond**

Client: **The McGraw-Hill Companies**
Design Firm: **Lippincott & Margulies**
Designers: **Connie Birdsall, Jane Ashley**

Client: **Tenneco**
Design Firm: **Lippincott & Margulies**
Designers: **Ken Love, Jane Bocker**

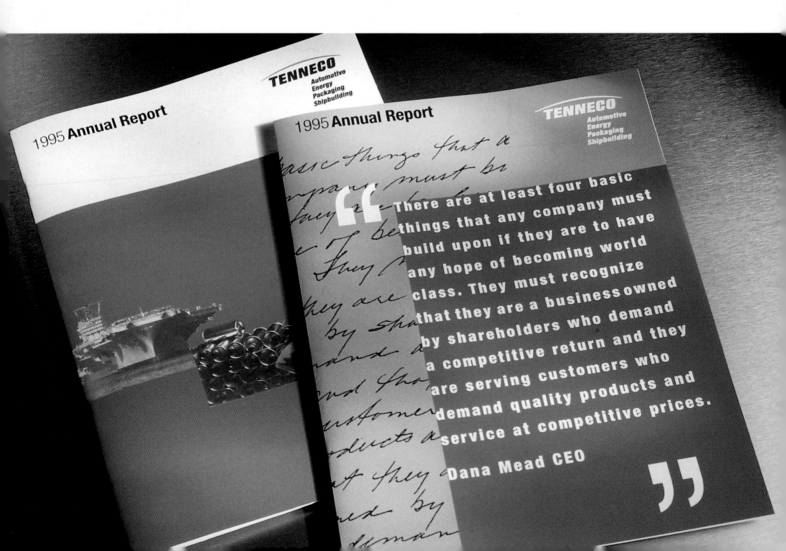

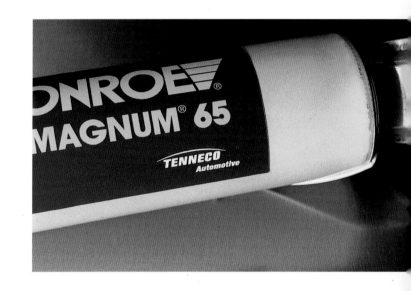

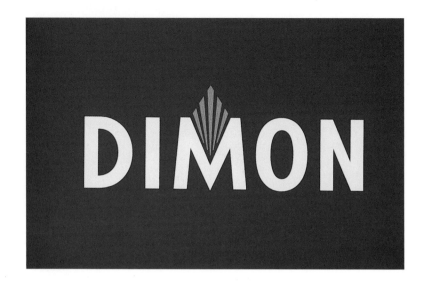

Client: **Dimon**
Design Firm: **Lippincott & Margulies**
Designers: **Ken Love, Ryan Paul**

CHARTWAY

FEDERAL CREDIT UNION

Client: **Chartway Financial Services**
Design Firm: **Lippincott & Margulies**
Designers: **Connie Birdsall, Gyeong Lee**

Client: **The Deloitte & Touche Consulting Group**
Design Firm: **Lippincott & Margulies**
Designers: **Rodney Abbot, Ken Love**

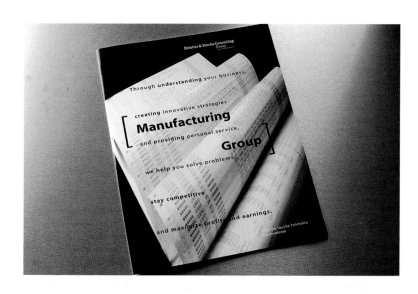

Client: **360**
Design Firm: **Siegel & Gale**
Designers: **Kenneth Cooke, Jerry Kuyper,**
Raul Gutierrez, George Ganginis, Eric Olson

Client: **A to Z Communications, Inc.**
Design Firm: **A to Z Communications, Inc.**
Designers: **Larkin Werner, Joe Tomko**

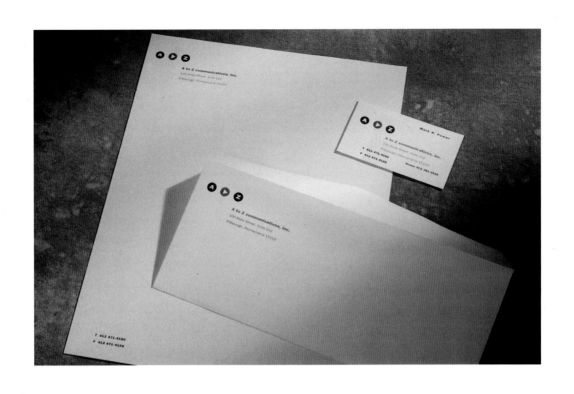

Client: **Advanced Network Technologies, Inc.**
Design Firm: **Cathey Associates, Inc.**
Designers: **Gordon Cathey, Craig Cathey,
Matt Westapher**

24

aerea

Client: **Aerea**
Design Firm: **Lawrence Design Group, Inc.**
Designer: **Marie-Christine Lawrence**

26

Client: **Airtouch**
Design Firm: **Addison Seefeld and Brew**
Designer: **John Creson**

AirTouch™
Communications

Client: **Ashland Petroleum**
Design Firm: **Antista Fairclough Design**
Designers: **Tom Antista, Thomas Fairclough**

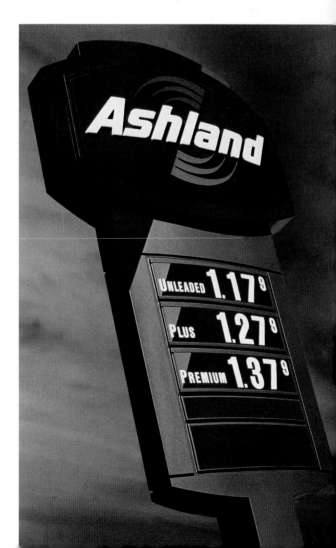

Client: **BRIAZZ**
Design Firm: **Tim Girvin Design, Inc.**
Designer: **Laurie Vette**

BUFFALO STATE COLLEGE

PERFORMING

ARTS CENTER

AT ROCKWELL HALL

Client: **Buffalo State Performing Arts Center**
Design Firm: **Crowley Webb and Associates**
Designer: **Rob Wynne**

34

Community Memorial Hospital

Client: **Community Memorial Hospital—Hicksville**
Design Firm: **Yvonne Dale Graphics**
Designers: **Yvonne Dale, Jill Evans**

CMH

A Team of
Caring Professionals
Dedicated
to Providing
Quality
Health Services
for Our Communities.

Community Memorial Hospital

CMH

CMH

Community Memorial Hospital
208 North Columbus Street
Hicksville, OH 43526
419.542.6692 or 1.800.686.6552

Your next appointment with
Date
Time

Community Memorial Hospital
208 North Columbus
Hicksville, Ohio 43526-1299
Tel 419.542.6692
Fax 419.542.6440

Community Memorial Hospital
208 North Columbus
Hicksville, Ohio 43526-1299
Tel 419.542.6692
Fax 419.542.6440

CMH

Client: **Drexel Heritage**
Design Firm: **Desgrippes Gobé & Associates**
Designers: **Phyllis Aragaki, Anne Swan**

Community Memorial Hospital

Client: **Community Memorial Hospital—Hicksville**
Design Firm: **Yvonne Dale Graphics**
Designers: **Yvonne Dale, Jill Evans**

Client: **Drexel Heritage**
Design Firm: **Desgrippes Gobé & Associates**
Designers: **Phyllis Aragaki, Anne Swan**

39

Client: **Alki Bakery and Cafe, Inc.**
Design Firm: **Hornall Anderson Design Works, Inc.**

Client: **Inacom Corporation**
Design Firm: **Profile Design**
Designers: **Jun Kidokoro, Kenichi Nishiwaki,
Brian Jacobson, Anthony Luk**

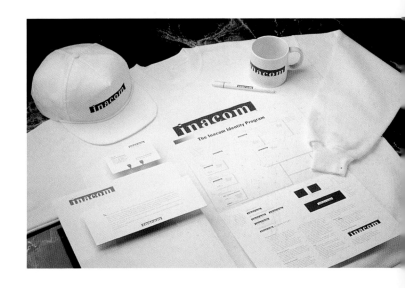

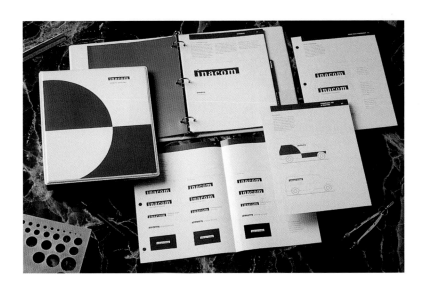

Client: **Lexis-Nexis**
Design Firm: **Graphica**
Designers: **Linda Sowers, Drew Cronenwett, Lisa Acup**

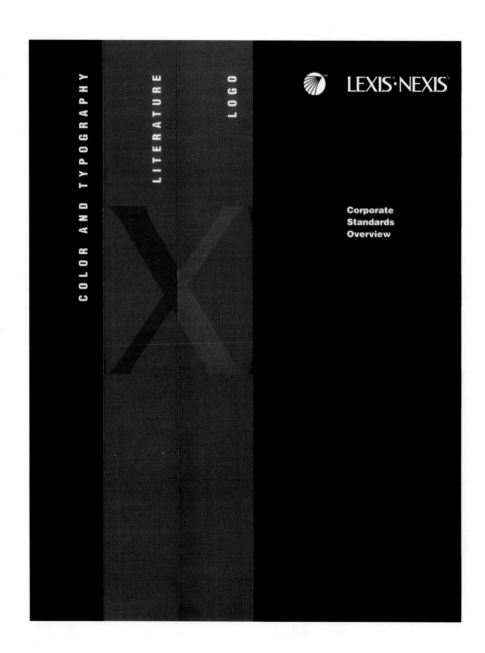

9443 Springboro Pike
P.O. Box 933
Dayton, Ohio 45401

LEXIS·NEXIS

A member of the Reed Elsevier plc group

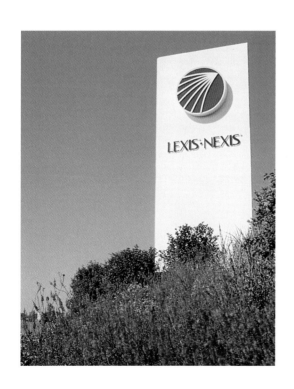

9443 Springboro Pike
P.O. Box 933
Dayton, Ohio 45401

LEXIS·NEXIS

Client: **NBC Desktop Video**
Design Firm: **Hadtke Design**
Designers: **Hadtke Staff, R. Karsten, C. Martinez**

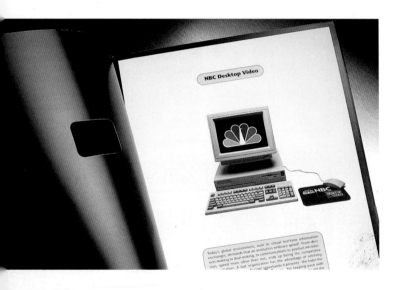

44

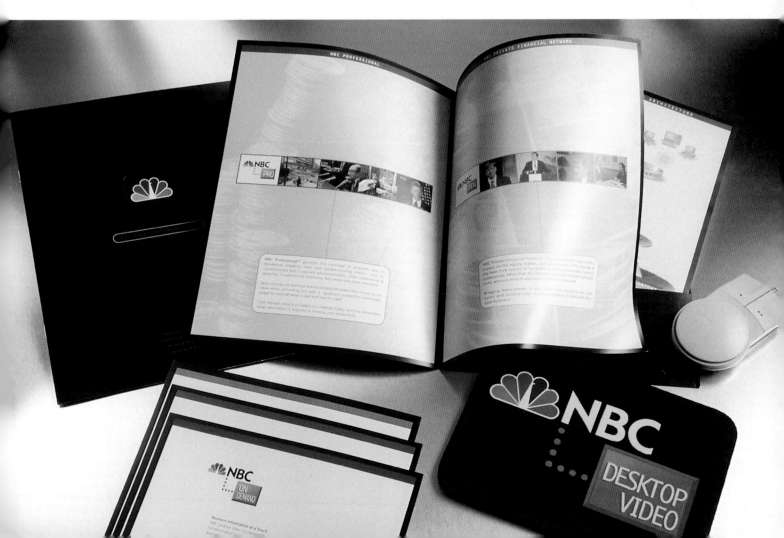

Client: **National Semiconductor**
Design Firm: **Siegel & Gale**
Designers: **Kenneth Cooke, Raul Gutierrez**

Client: **MCI Prepaid Card Marketing**
Design Firm: **Degnen Associates, Inc.**
Designers: **Stephen Degnen, Mark Denzer,**
  David Fowler, Wendy Burkin

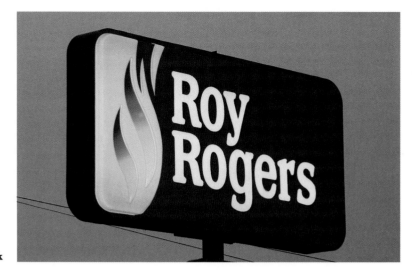

Client: **Roy Rogers**
Design Firm: **King Casey, Inc.**
Designers: **John Chrzanowski, Christen Kucharik**

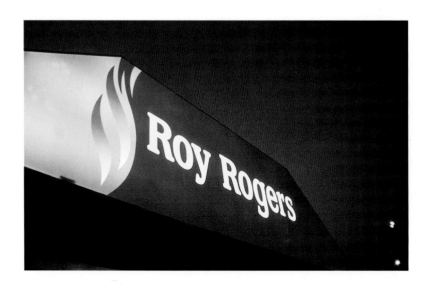

50

Client: **Sizzler International**
Design Firm: **King Casey, Inc.**
Designers: **John Chrzanowski, Jean Perlesch,
Jeff Redston**

Client: **Ann Taylor Loft**
Design Firm: **Desgrippes Gobé & Associates**
Designers: **Peter Levine, Kim Týska**

Client: **Timbuktuu Coffee Bar**
Design Firm: **Sayles Graphic Design**
Designer: **John Sayles**

Client: **Van Bloem, Inc.**
Design Firm: **Gerstman + Meyers, Inc.**
Designer: **Chris Sanders**

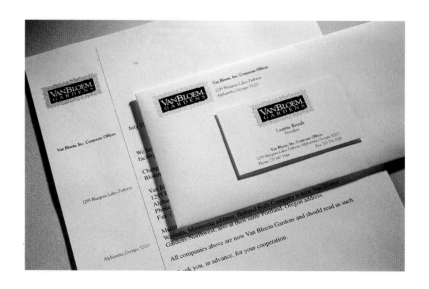

58

Package Designs

Client: **The J.M. Smucker's Co.**
Design Firm: **Landor Associates**
Designer: **Bill Chiaravalle**

Client: **Gatorade**
Design Firm: **Landor Associates**
Designers: **Jon Weden, Randy Fisher**

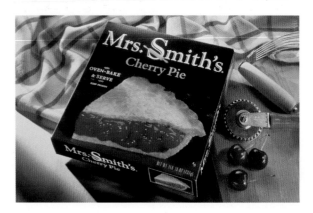

Client: **Oral-B**
Design Firm: **Landor Associates**
Designer: **Jeff Pascoe, Nat Plummanus**

Client: **Mrs Smith's**
Design Firm: **Landor Associates**
Designer: **Bill Chiaravalle**

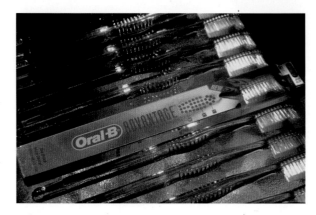

Client: **Sutter Home Winery**
Design Firm: **Landor Associates**
Designer: **Peter Matsukawa**

Client: **Brita**
Design Firm: **Landor Associates**
Designers: **Jeff Pascoe, Randy Fisher,
Nat Plummanus, Ariel Villasol**

Client: **DelMonte**
Design Firm: **Landor Associates**
Designer: **Serena Wong**

Client: **H.E.B. Grocery**
Design Firm: **Landor Associates**
Designers: **Jon Weden Michael Livolsi, Quentin Murley**

Client: **Dreyer's**
Design Firm: **Landor Associates**
Designers: **Jon Weden, Ariel Villasol**

Client: **Foster Farms, Inc.**
Design Firm: **Landor Associates**
Designer: **Randy Fisher**

Client: **IBM—children's software**
Design Firm: **Lippincott & Margulies**
Designers: **Connie Birdsall, Rodney Abbot**

Client: **Keebler Company—pretzels**
Design Firm: **Harbauer/Bruce Design, Ltd.**
Designers: **Steve Walker, Annette Ohlsen**

Client: **Inoxpran**
Design Firm: **Zen Design Firm**
Designers: **David Yee, Paul Burke**

Client: **CBT Systems USA, Ltd.**
Design Firm: **Three Marketeers Advertising, Inc.**
Designers: **Jeff Holmes, Greg Campbell,**
Amelia Rodrigues, Tracy Power

Client: **Old Dutch Foods**
Design Firm: **Creative Resource Center**
Designers: **Keith Anderson, Tom Dierberger**

Client: **Playcrest Industries**
Design Firm: **Zen Design Group**
Designer: **Paul Burke**

Client: **GUESS? Inc.**
Design Firm: **GUESS? In-House Designers**
Designers: **Kumiko Morishita, Vicki Sum**

Client: **Terramar Sports Worldwide, Ltd.**
Design Firm: **Hothouse Designs, Inc.**
Designers: **Brian Sheridan, Glen Hagen**

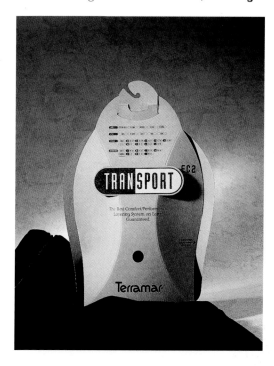

Client: **American Popcorn Company**
Design Firm: **Dixon & Parcels Assoc.**
Designers: **Dixon & Parcels Assoc.**

Client: **General Electric Co.**
Design Firm: **Zen Design Group**
Designers: **Sun Yu, Paul Burke**

Client: **I. Shalom & Co., Inc.**
Design Firm: **By Design**
Designer: **John Hnath**

Client: **GM Service Parts Operations**
Design Firm: **General Motors Design**
Designers: **Joann Kallio**

Client: **Go Sportsman Supply—A-Square**
Design Firm: **Advertising Design, Inc.**
Designers: **Eric Finstad, Steven Squire**

Client: **Federal Cartridge**
Design Firm: **MVP—Marketing, Visuals &**
Promotion, Inc.
Designers: **Linda Okan, Dick Weinrib**

Client: **Federal Cartridge**
Design Firm: **MVP—Marketing, Visuals &**
Promotion, Inc.
Designers: **Linda Okan, Dick Weinrib**

64

Client: **Johnny Mash Hard Cider**
Design Firm: **Upland Advertising**
Designer: **Art White**

Client: **SC Johnson Wax—Drano Clog Remover**
Design Firm: **The Weber Group, Inc.**
Designers: **Anthony T. Weber, Pat Cowan**

Client: **Cacique, Inc.—Yonique**
Design Firm: **Acento Advertising, Inc.**
Designer: **Alex Mayans**

Client: **Scholastic**
Design Firm: **1185 Design**
Designers: **Nhuy Nguyen, Peggy Burke**

Client: **Stanford Business School**
Design Firm: **1185 Design**
Designers: **Nhuy Nguyen, Peggy Burke**

Client: **Amazonia**
Design Firm: **PJ Graphics**
Designers: **Paula Menchen,**
Justin Menchen

Client: **Twin Palms Restaurant**
Design Firm: **McNulty & Co.**
Designer: **Jennifer McNulty**

Client: **Thiébaud & Cie, Switzerland**
Design Firm: **Hans Flink Design, Inc.**
Designers: **Hans Flink, Harry Bertschmann,**
Steve Hooper, Chang Mei Lin

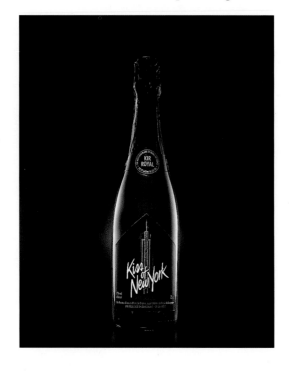

Client: **Mendocino Brewing Company**
Design Firm: **William Bell & Company**
Designer: **William Bell**

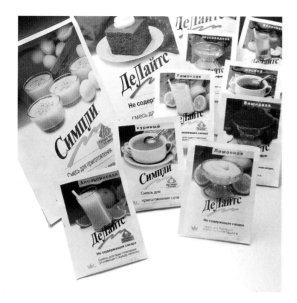

Client: **Crown Laboratories, Inc.**
Design Firm: **The Design Center**
Designers: **Janet McComas, Wayne Bandur**

Client: **4C Foods Corporation**
Raspberry Iced Tea Mix
Design Firm: **Dixon & Parcels Assoc., Inc.**
Designers: **Dixon & Parcels Assoc., Inc.**

Client: **4C Foods Corporation**
Raspberry Iced Tea
Design Firm: **Dixon & Parcels Assoc., Inc.**
Designers: **Dixon & Parcels Assoc., Inc.**

Client: **Stokes Ellis Foods**
Design Firm: **The Design Center**
Designer: **Janet McComas**

Client: **Nordic Software**
Design Firm: **Muller + Company**
Designers: **Jon Simonsen,
David Shultz**

Client: **BB Entertainment**
Design Firm: **Adkins/Balchunas Design**
Designer: **Jerry Balchunas**

Client: **SC Johnson Wax—Shout Carpet Cleaner**
Design Firm: **The Weber Group, Inc.**
Designers: **Anthony T. Weber, Jeffrey A. Tischer**

Client: **International Playthings**
Design Firm: **Studio Izbickas**
Designer: **Edmund Izbickas**

Client: **The Gillette Company**
Gillette Satin Care Shave Gel
Design Firm: **Wallace Church Associates, Inc.**
Designers: **Stan Church, John Waski**

Client: **DowBrands Salon Division**
CLER haircare product line
Design Firm: **Rapp Collins Communications**
Designer: **Bruce Edwards**

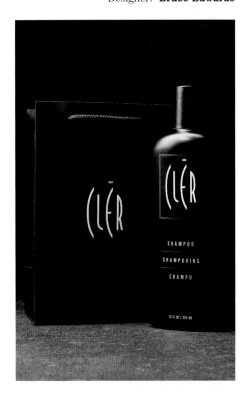

Client: **Johnson & Johnson**
Clean & Clear
Design Firm: **Bailey Design Group**
Designer: **Steve Perry**

Client: **Supre, Inc.—Impact**
Design Firm: **Swieter Design United States**
Designers: **John Swieter,**
Mark Ford, Jenice Heo

Client: **William B. Reilly Co.—JFG Coffee**
Design Firm: **Gerstman + Meyers, Inc.**
Designer: **Jeff Zack**

Client: **Kraft Foods—Gevalia Royal Vinter Caffe**
Design Firm: **Muts & Joy & Design**
Designer: **Katherine Hames**

Client: **Kraft Foods—Gevalia Island Mountain Caffe**
Design Firm: **Muts & Joy & Design**
Designer: **Katherine Hames**

Client: **Kraft Foods—Café de Oriente (Spain)**
Design Firm: **Muts & Joy & Design**
Designer: **Gisele Sangiovanni**

Client: **Kraft Foods—Café Rapperswil (Swiss)**
Design Firm: **Muts & Joy & Design**
Designer: **Katherine Hames**

Client: **World of Peace**
Design Firm: **The Appelbaum Company**
Designer: **Harvey Appelbaum, Nick Guarracino**

Client: **Chippewa Springs, Ltd.**
Design Firm: **Hillis Mackey & Company**
Designer: **Jim Hillis**

Client: **Torani Syrups for R. Torre**
Design Firm: **Primo Angeli, Inc.**
Designers: **Rich Scheve, Primo Angeli, Carlo Pagoda**

Client: **SLM—Bitsy Buddies**
Design Firm: **Designed to Print**
Designer: **Peggy Leonard, Tree Trapanese, David Un**

Client: **Alpha Enterprises—Keeparoo's**
Design Firm: **Louis & Partners**
Designers: **Louis & Partners**

Client: **Cory Cafe**
Design Firm: **Bailey Design Group**
Designer: **Wendy Seldomridge**

Client: **No-Snore**
Design Firm: **Phoenix Creative, St. Louis**
Designers: **Ed Mantels-Seeker,
Eric Thoelke**

Client: **Black Mountain Brewing Co.—Bighorn Bock**
Design Firm: **Tieken Design & Creative Services**
Designers: **Fred E. Tieken, Rik Boberg**

Client: **EQ—Environmental Quality Company**
Design Firm: **Mars Advertising**
Designers: **Michele Vredevoogd, Susan Sanderson**

Client: **Black Mountain Brewing Co.
Juanderful Weizen**
Design Firm: **Tieken Design & Creative Services**
Designers: **Fred E. Tieken, Rik Boberg**

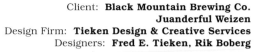

Client: **Doubletree Hotel Lax**
Design Firm: **The Wecker Group**
Designers: **Robert J. Wecker, Matt Gnibus**

Client: **The Vein Center**
Design Firm: **Phoenix Creative, St. Louis**
Designer: **Ed Mantels-Seeker**

Client: **Black Mountain Brewing Co.**
Cerveza de Cantina
Design Firm: **Tieken Design & Creative Services**
Designers: **Fred E. Tieken, Tad A. Smith**

Client: **Anheuser Busch**
Design Firm: **Phoenix Creative, St. Louis**
Designers: **Kathy Wilkinson, Eric Thoelke**

Client: **L&A Juice Company**
Kid's Line
Design Firm: **Bright & Associates**
Designer: **Bill Corridori**

Client: **Hasbro Toy Group—Secret Beauties**
Design Firm: **Designed to Print**
Designers: **Tree Trapanese, David Un, Peggy Leonard**

Client: **Toybiz—Gerber Electronic Infant Line**
Design Firm: **Designed to Print**
Designers: **Tree Trapanese, Peggy Leonard, David Un**

Client: **Toybiz—Caboodles Jeweled Line**
Design Firm: **Designed to Print**
Designers: **Tree Trapanese, Peggy Leonard, David Un**

Client: **Cadbury Beverages**
Design Firm: **Hans Flink Design, Inc.**
Designers: **Hans Flink, Denise Heisey,
Chang-Mei Lin**

Client: **Hasbro Toy Group—Real Power Toolshop**
Design Firm: **Designed to Print**
Designers: **Tree Trapanese, David Un, Peggy Leonard**

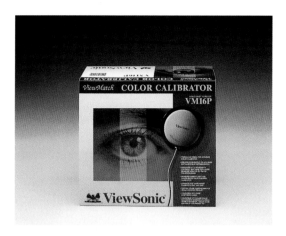

Client: **ViewSonic Corp.—Color Calibrator Box**
Design Firm: **Artime, Crane & Company**
Designers: **Henry Artime, Denver Minnich, Tricia Wiley**

Client: **VLSI Technology**
Design Firm: **Wynn Art Direction**
Designer: **Christopher Wynn**

Client: **Imagery Software, Inc.**
Design Firm: **Gill Fishman Assoc., Inc.**
Designer: **Michael Persons**

Client: **Prestone Products Corporation—Bug Wash**
Design Firm: **HMS Design**
Designer: **Paul Beichert**

Client: **Prestone Products Corporation—Professional Clean**
Design Firm: **HMS Design**
Designer: **Mary Ellen Butkus**

Client: **Pelco**
Design Firm: **Parola Design**
Designer: **Michael Parola**

Client: **Alberto-Culver Company**
Design Firm: **JOED Design**
Designers: **Ed Rebek, Joanne Rebek**

Client: **Tradeglobe—Converse Basketballs**
Design Firm: **Swieter Design United States**
Designers: **Kevin Flatt, Paul Munsterman, John Swieter**

Client: **Joseph E. Seagram & Sons**
Design Firm: **Kollberg/Johnson Associates**
Designers: **Penny Johnson, Michael Carr**

Client: **Silore, division of Essilor of America, Inc. Thin & Lite**
Design Firm: **Lee Communications, Inc.**
Designers: **Bob Lee, Dennis Defrancesco**

Client: **Seagram's**
Design Firm: **Port Miolla Associates**
Designer: **Jennifer Abramson**

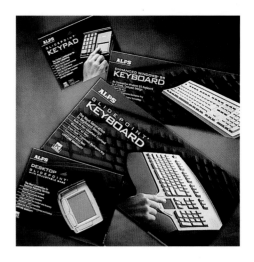

Client: **Alps Electric**
Design Firm: **Monnens-Addis Design**
Designers: **Rick Atwood, Leila Daubert,**
   James Eli, Trevor Wright

Client: **Twin County Grocers, Inc.**
Design Firm: **Berni Design**
Designers: **Berni Design**

Client: **Safeway Stores**
Design Firm: **Profile Design**
Designers: **Tom McNulty, Jeanne Namkung**

Client: **Briazz**
Design Firm: **Tim Girvin Design, Inc.**
Designers: **Laurie Vette, Tim Girvin,**
   Craig McBreen, Kathy Saito

Client: **Perdue Farms, Inc.—Short Cuts**
Design Firm: **Gerstman + Meyers, Inc.**
Designers: **Larry Riddell, Diane Sheridan**

Client: **The Stop & Shop Supermarket Co.**
Design Firm: **Berni Design**
Designers: **Berni Design**

Client: **Southland Corporation**
Design Firm: **Nexus,
A Design Group, Inc.**
Designer: **Bill Ward**

Client: **Laurel Glen Vineyard**
Design Firm: **Buttitta Design**
Designer: **Lisa Hobro**

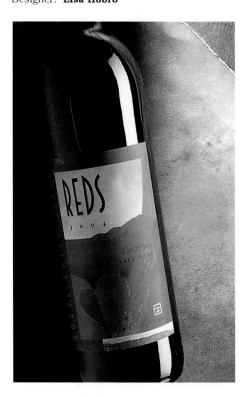

Client: **Red River for Hal Riney and Partners**
Design Firm: **Primo Angeli, Inc.**
Designers: **Mark Jones, Jerry Andelin,
Primo Angeli**

Client: **Foote, Cone + Belding for Adolph Coors Brewing Co.**
Design Firm: **Primo Angeli, Inc.**
Designers: **Carlo Pagoda, Marcelo De Freitas, Primo Angeli,
Rolando Rosler, Brody Hartman, George Chadwick**

78

Client: **Joseph E. Seagram & Sons**
Design Firm: **Kollberg/Johnson Associates**
Designer: **Peter Johnson**

Client: **Heublin, Inc.**
Design Firm: **Hughes Design**
Designers: **Barney Hughes, Siri Korsgren**

Client: **Great Brands of Europe**
Design Firm: **Port Miolla Associates**
Designer: **Robert Swan**

Client: **Jim Beam Brands**
DeKuyper Mad Melon
Design Firm: **Di Donato Associates**
Designer: **Don Childs**

Client: **Mont Source—cologne tins**
Design Firm: **Antista Fairclough Design**
Designers: **Tom Antista, Thomas Fairclough**

Client: **Chesebrough-Pond's—Actif Blue**
Design Firm: **Port Miolla Associates**
Designer: **Robert Swan**

Client: **The Gillette Company—Pacific Light**
Design Firm: **Wallace Church Associates, Inc.**
Designers: **Stan Church, John Waski**

Client: **SmithKline Beecham—Contac Cold & Flu**
Design Firm: **Wallace Church Associates, Inc.**
Designers: **Stan Church, Phyllis Chan-Carr**

Client: **Warner Wellcome**
Design Firm: **Monnens-Addis Design**
Designers: **Rick Atwood, Storey Jones, David Leong,
James Eli, Tin Chu, Shirley Ng-Benitez, David Campbell**

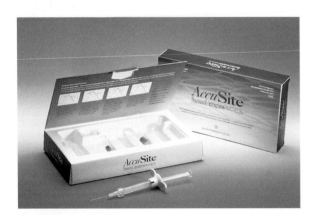

Client: **Matrix Pharmaceutical, Inc.**
Design Firm: **Artemis**
Designers: **Stacie Baptist, Laura Medeiros,
Terry Monaco**

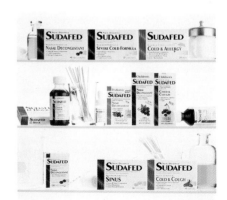

Client: **Sterling Software, Inc.**
Design Firm: **Quill Creative, Inc.**
Designer: **Steve Utley**

Client: **Harman Kardon International**
Design Firm: **Fitch, Inc.**
Designers: **Jeff Pacione, Ellen Hartshorne,**
Ben Segal, Art Tran

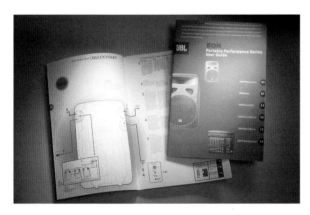

Client: **Sony Music Entertainment**
Design Firm: **Watts Design?**
Designer: **Michael Boland**

Client: **Genisis Direct**
Design Firm: **The Madison Group**
Designers: **Susan Edinger, Dana Miller**

Client: **Copper Development Association**
Design Firm: **Lee Communications, Inc.**
Designers: **Bob Lee, Dennis Defrancesco**

Client: **NetSuite**
Design Firm: **The Selig Group**
Designers: **Jean Resteghini, Maria DiGioia**

Client: **Austin Quality Foods, Inc.**
    Lemon-Burst Sugar Cookies
Design Firm: **Dixon & Parcels Assoc., Inc.**
Designers: **Dixon & Parcels Assoc., Inc.**

Client: **Baskin Robbins**
Design Firm: **DuPuis**
Designer: **Steven DuPuis**

Client: **Austin Quality Foods, Inc.**
    Cheddar Crackers
Design Firm: **Dixon & Parcels Assoc., Inc.**
Designers: **Dixon & Parcels Assoc., Inc.**

Client: **Kraft Foods**
Design Firm: **Tim Girvin Design, Inc.**
Designers: **Tim Girvin, Paulette Subert**

Client: **Jardine's Classics Dressings**
Design Firm: **Bailey Design Group**
Designer: **Ken Cahill**

Client: **Mezcal Importers, Inc.**
Design Firm: **Banks & Associates**
Designer: **Lionel Banks**

Client: **Cacique, Inc.**
Mex-Tex Classic Brand
Design Firm: **Acento Advertising**
Designer: **Auejandro Mayans**

Client: **Stokes Ellis Foods**
Design Firm: **The Design Center**
Designer: **Jim Erlander**

Client: **Comstock Michigan Fruit Division**
Orchard Farm Pie
Design Firm: **McElveney & Palozzi Design Group**
Designers: **William M. McElveney, Stephen Palozzi**

Client: **Comstock Michigan Fruit Division**
Comstock More Fruit
Design Firm: **Gerstman + Meyers, Inc.**
Designers: **Gerstman + Meyers, Inc.**

Client: **Guggisberg Cheese**
Design Firm: **Louis & Partners**
Designers: **Louis & Partners**

Client: **Vitamin Healthcenters**
Design Firm: **The Design Company**
Designers: **Alison Scheel, Marcia Romanuck**

Client: **G + G Foods**
Design Firm: **Auston Design Group**
Designers: **Tony Auston, Mike Gray, Jeanne Greco**

84

Client: **Schwebel's Baking—Country Potato Bread**
Design Firm: **Di Donato Associates**
Designer: **Don Childs**

Client: **Pacific Grain Products**
Design Firm: **Thompson Design Group**
Designer: **Dawn Janney**

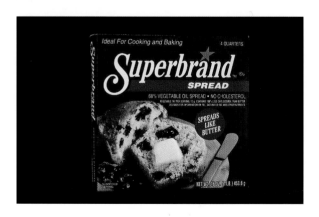

Client: **Deep South Products, Inc.—Superbrand Spread**
Design Firm: **Dixon & Parcels Assoc., Inc.**
Designers: **Dixon & Parcels Assoc., Inc.**

Client: **Trader Joes**
Design Firm: **Vince Rini Design**
Designer: **Vince Rini**

Client: **Kraft Foods, Inc.**
Design Firm: **Hughes Design**
Designers: **Barney Hughes, Siri Korsgren**

Client: **Trader Joes**
Design Firm: **Vince Rini Design**
Designer: **Vince Rini**

Client: **Boisset USA**
Design Firm: **Cahan & Associates**
Designer: **Sharrie Brooks**

Client: **Magic Hat Brewing Company**
Design Firm: **Jager Di Paola Kemp Design**
Designers: **Michael Jager, David Covell**

Client: **Anheuser Busch—Michelob Golden Light**
Design Firm: **Antista Fairclough Design**
Designers: **Tom Antista, Thomas Fairclough**

Client: **Anheuser Busch—Crossroads**
Design Firm: **Antista Fairclough Design**
Designers: **Tom Antista, Thomas Fairclough**

Client: **Anheuser Busch—Anheuser Light**
Design Firm: **Antista Fairclough Design**
Designers: **Tom Antista, Thomas Fairclough**

Client: **Kirin Lite**
Design Firm: **Bright & Associates**
Designer: **Ray Wood**

Client: **Krypto International, Inc.**
Max Beck Design
Design Firm: **Axioma, Inc.**
Designer: **José Bila Rodriguez**

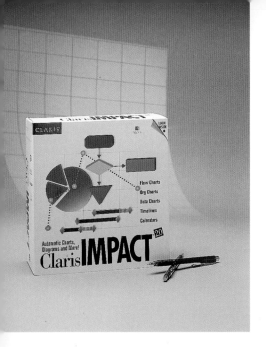

Client: **Claris Corporation**
Design Firm: **Bonnie Smetts Design**
Designer: **Bonnie Smetts**

Design Firm: **"IN-HOUSE"**
Seasonal Specialities Electrics
Designer: **Barbara Roth**

Client: **Revelation Technologies**
Design Firm: **Corporate Branding Partnership**
Designer: **Michael Glass**

Client: **Timex—Joe Boxer**
Design Firm: **Smart Design, Inc.**
Designers: **Tucker Viemeister, Debbie Hahn,**
Stephanie Kim, Nick Graham

Client: **Fabergé Co.**
Design Firm: **Hans Flink Design, Inc.**
Designers: **Chang Mei Lin, Hans Flink, Mel Abfier**

Client: **Dow Brands Salon Division**
Nucleic A Haircare Products
Design Firm: **Rapp Collins Communications**
Designer: **Bruce Edwards**

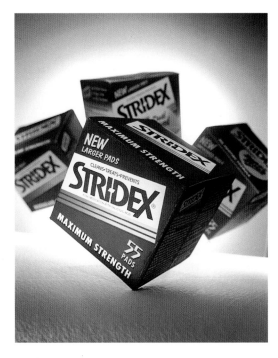

Client: **Bayer Corporation**
Design Firm: **Hans Flink Design, Inc.**
Designers: **Hans Flink, Chang Mei Lin,**
Stephen Hooper

Client: **Alberto Culver**
Design Firm: **Hans Flink Design, Inc.**
Designers: **Hans Flink, Mark Krukonis**

Client: **Taco Bell**
Design Firm: **Axion Design**
Designer: **Eric Read**

Client: **Sara Lee**
Design Firm: **Axion Design**
Designer: **Kenn Lewis**

Client: **Multifoods, Inc.**
Design Firm: **MVP—Marketing, Visuals & Promotions**
Designers: **Linda Okan, Dick Weinrib**

Client: **Simply Caribbean**
Design Firm: **Caldewey Design**
Designer: **Jeffrey Caldewey**

Client: **Staley Vineyards**
Design Firm: **The Van Noy Design Group**
Designers: **Bill Murawski, Jim Van Noy**

Client: **Charles Krug Winery**
Design Firm: **Caldewey Design**
Designer: **Jeffrey Caldewey**

Client: **Zia Cellars**
Design Firm: **Caldewey Design**
Designer: **Jeffrey Caldewey**

Client: **Boisset USA**
Design Firm: **Caldewey Design**
Designer: **Jeffrey Caldewey**

Client: **Godiva Chocolatier, Inc.**
Design Firm: **J K Designs, Inc.**
Designers: **John R. Kocum,
Stephanie Witham**

Client: **McGlynn's Bakery—Renaissance Breads**
Design Firm: **Creative Resource Center**
Designers: **Tom Nelson, Liz Petrangelo**

Client: **Fran's Chocolates**
Design Firm: **Walsh and Associates, Inc.**
Designers: **Miriam Lisco, Michael Stearns**

Client: **Chukar Cherries**
Design Firm: **Walsh and Associates, Inc.**
Designer: **Miriam Lisco**

Client: **Nabisco Foods, Inc.**
Design Firm: **Haber Design Group**
Designers: **Lee Haber, Eileen Strauss**

Client: **Heidel's Famous Foods, Inc.
Heidel House Salad Dressing**
Design Firm: **The Weber Group, Inc.**
Designers: **Jeffrey A. Tischer, Anthony T. Weber**

Client: **Victoria's Secret Fragrances**
Design Firm: **J K Designs, Inc.**
Designer: **John R. Kocum**

Client: **Susan Ciminelli Day Spa**
Design Firm: **J K Designs, Inc.**
Designers: **John R. Kocum, Stephanie Witham**

Client: **Chesebrough Pond International**
Design Firm: **Hans Flink Design, Inc.**
Designers: **Chang-Mei Lin, Hans Flink**

Client: **Motorola—Compass**
Design Firm: **Vaughn Wedeen Creative, Inc.**
Designer: **Daniel Michael Flynn**

Client: **S.C. Johnson & Son, Inc.—Edge After Shave**
Design Firm: **The Weber Group, Inc.**
Designers: **Anthony T. Weber, Pat Cowan**

Client: **Rovar Soaps**
Design Firm: **McNulty & Co.**
Designers: **Dan McNulty, Ben Lopez**

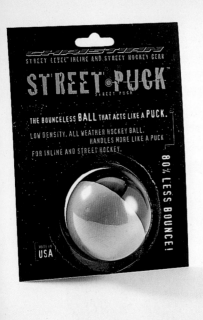

Client: **Christian Brothers**
Design Firm: **PLD**
Designer: **Chris Adams**

Client: **Captoys, Inc.—Katie Kiss 'n' Giggles**
Design Firm: **Designed to Print**
Designers: **Peggy Leonard, Tree Trapanese**

Client: **Toybiz—Gerber Collector Doll**
Design Firm: **Designed to Print**
Designers: **Tree Trapanese, Peggy Leonard, David Un**

Client: **Captoys, Inc.—Bundle of Babies**
Design Firm: **Designed to Print**
Designers: **Tree Trapanese, Peggy Leonard**

Client: **Blue Mountain Beverage Co.**
Design Firm: **Auston Design Group**
Designers: **Tony Auston, Jeanne Greco**

Client: **Osprey**
Design Firm: **Guttman Design**
Designers: **Suzanne Guttman, Tony Auston,
Steven Perringer**

Client: **G. Heileman Brewing Co.—Henry Weinhard's Root Beer**
Design Firm: **Primo Angeli, Inc.**
Designers: **Mark Jones, Brody Hartman, Carlo Pagoda, Primo Angeli**

Client: **Pokka, Inc.**
Design Firm: **Profile Design**
Designers: **Kenichi Nishiwaki, Jeanne Namkung**

Client: **Nestlé Beverage Company—Carnation Hot Cocoa**
Design Firm: **Primo Angeli, Inc.**
Designers: **Nina Dietzel, Mark Jones,
Primo Angeli, Rolando Rosler**

Client: **Welch's JuiceMakers**
Design Firm: **Bailey Design Group**
Designers: **Dave Fiedler, Laura Markley**

Client: **Nordic Advantage, Inc.**
Design Firm: **PLD**
Designer: **Chris Adams**

Client: **Alpha Cool Colors**
Design Firm: **Louis & Partners**
Designers: **Louis & Partners**

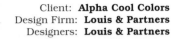

Client: **The Hayes Co., Inc.—Sunflower Garden**
Design Firm: **Love Packaging Group**
Designers: **Tracy Holdeman, Brian Miller**

Client: **The Hayes Co., Inc.**
   American Garden Collection
Design Firm: **Love Packaging Group**
Designer: **Tracy Holdeman**

Client: **Borai Bricks, Inc.**
Design Firm: **The Crosby Agency**
Designer: **Bruce Clifton**

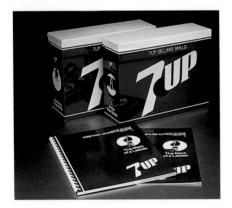

Client: **The Seven-Up Company**
Design Firm: **Cathey Associates, Inc.**
Designer: **Gordon Cathey**

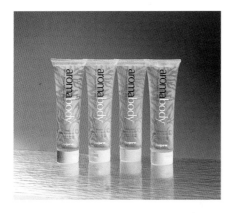

Client: **Supre, Inc.—Aromabody Shower Gels**
Design Firm: **Swieter Design United States**
Designers: **Jenice Heo, John Swieter**

Client: **Scott Paper Company**
Cottonelle Bathroom Tissue
Design Firm: **Wallace Church Associates, Inc.**
Designers: **Stan Church, Phyllis Chan-Carr**

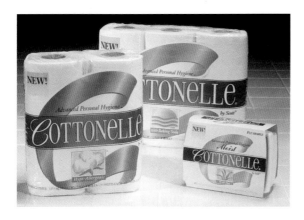

Client: **Georgia-Pacific Corporation**
Georgia Pacific Papers
Design Firm: **Gerstman + Meyers, Inc.**
Designer: **Diane Sheridan**

Client: **Chesebrough-Pond's USA Co.**
Prevent & Correct
Design Firm: **Tom Fowler, Inc.**
Designers: **Elizabeth P. Ball, Samuel Toh**

Client: **SC Johnson Wax**
Professional Cleaning Products
Design Firm: **The Weber Group, Inc.**
Designers: **Anthony T. Weber, Cody Hudson, Pat Cowan**

Client: **United States Postal Service**
Design Firm: **The Madison Group**
Designer: **Yoshifumi Fujii**

Client: **Heublin, Inc.**
Design Firm: **Kollberg/Johnson Associates**
Designers: **Kollberg/Johnson**

Client: **Labatt USA—Labatt Blue 24-Pack**
Design Firm: **Muts & Joy & Design**
Designer: **Akira Otani**

Client: **Goose Island Brewery—Honker's Ale**
Design Firm: **Di Donato Associates**
Designer: **Don Childs**

Client: **Anheuser Busch—American Originals
Black and Tan**
Design Firm: **Antista Fairclough Design**
Designers: **Tom Antista, Thomas Fairclough**

Client: **Anheuser Busch—Busch NA Secondary**
Design Firm: **Antista Fairclough Design**
Designers: **Tom Antista, Thomas Fairclough**

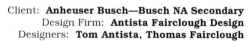

98

Client: **Anheuser Busch**
  American Originals Muenchener
Design Firm: **Antista Fairclough Design**
Designers: **Tom Antista, Thomas Fairclough**

Client: **Rhino Chasers**
Design Firm: **Hornall Anderson Design Works, Inc.**
Designers: **Jack Anderson, Larry Anderson,**
John Hornall, Bruce Branson-Meyer

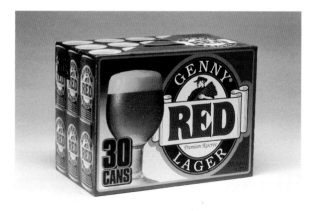

Client: **Genesee Brewing Company**
  Genny Red 30-Pack
Design Firm: **McElveney & Palozzi Graphic Design Group**
Designer: **Matthew Nowicki**

Client: **Labatt USA—Rolling Rock 12-Pack**
Design Firm: **Muts & Joy & Design**
Designer: **Akira Otani**

Client: **Anheuser Busch—American Originals Faust**
Design Firm: **Antista Fairclough Design**
Designers: **Tom Antista, Thomas Fairclough**

Client: **Samuel Adams—Boston Beer Co.**
Design Firm: **Muts & Joy & Design**
Designer: **Akira Otani**

Client: **GT Bicycles**
Bear Trap Pedals
Design Firm: **Rieches Baird**
Designer: **Carrie Sandoval**

Client: **Mont Source—cologne bottles**
Design Firm: **Antista Fairclough Design**
Designers: **Tom Antista, Thomas Fairclough**

Client: **Schick—FX Performer Razor**
Design Firm: **Muts & Joy & Design**
Designer: **Katherine Hames**

Client: **Alberto-Culver Company**
Design Firm: **JOED Design**
Designers: **Ed Rebek, Joanne Rebek**

Client: **Napa Valley Coffee Roasting, Co.**
Design Firm: **Auston Design Firm**
Designers: **Tony Auston, Mike Gray**

Client: **Carver's Ginger Ale**
Design Firm: **Robert Michael Communications, Inc.**
Designers: **Bob Colleluori, Robert M. Colleluori,
Kate Humes**

Client: **Welch's Sparkling
Grape Juice**
Design Firm: **Bailey Design Group**
Designer: **David Matthai**

Client: **Vitantonio Mfg.**
Mickey Mouse Popper
Design Firm: **Karen Skunta & Company**
Designer: **Karen A. Skunta**

Client: **OXO International**
Design Firm: **Hornall Anderson Design Works, Inc.**
Designers: **Jack Anderson, John Anicker, Heidi Favour, David Bates, Eulah Sheffield**

Client: **Corning, Inc.—Casual Elegance**
Design Firm: **Gerstman + Meyers, Inc.**
Designer: **Jeff Zack**

Client: **Eastman Kodak Company**
Celebration Edition
Design Firm: **McElveney & Palozzi Design Group**
Designers: **Jonathan Westfall, William M. McElveney**

Client: **Eastman Kodak Company—Kodak STAR**
Design Firm: **McElveney & Palozzi Design Group**
Designer: **Jonathan Westfall**

Client: **Eastman Kodak Company**
Kodak Olympic Cameo
Design Firm: **McElveney & Palozzi Design Group**
Designer: **Jonathan Westfall**

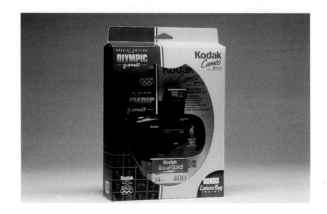

Client: **Samsung**
Design Firm: **Port Miolla Associates**
Designer: **Ralph Miolla**

Client: **Bil-Jac Foods, Inc.**
Design Firm: **Babcock & Schmid Associates, Inc.**
Designers: **Babcock & Schmid Associates, Inc.**

Client: **Goodyear-F-1 Racing 1994**
  "Down to the Wire"
Design Firm: **Herip Design Associates, Inc.**
Designers: **John R. Menter, Walter M. Herip**

Client: **GT Bicycles—Crankset**
Design Firm: **Rieches Baird Advertising**
Designer: **Carrie Sandoval**

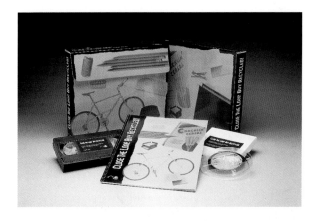

Client: **Keep America Beautiful, Inc.**
Design Firm: **Taylor Design**
Designers: **Daniel Taylor, Linda Frawley**

Client: **Sony Electronics, Inc.**
Design Firm: **Sony Design Center**
Designer: **Rosaline L. Yin**

Client: **Microrim**
Design Firm: **Hansen Design Company**
Designers: **Pat Hansen, Kip Henrie**

Client: **Megahertz Corporation**
Design Firm: **Hornall Anderson Design Works, Inc.**
Designers: **Julia LaPine, Jill Bustamante,
Bruce Branson-Meyer, Heidi Favour**

Client: **Iomega Corporation**
Design Firm: **Fitch, Inc.**
Designers: **Jaimie Alexander, Kate Murphy,
Eric Weissinger, Paul Lycett**

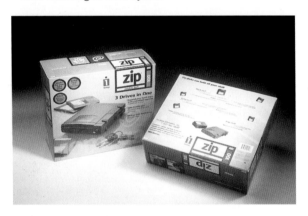

Client: **Digital Equipment Corporation**
Design Firm: **Fitch, Inc.**
Designers: **Robert Wood, Tammie Hunt,
Ellen Hartshorne, Carolina Senior, Brooks Beisch**

Client: **Ascend Communications, Inc.**
Design Firm: **Profile Design**
Designers: **Russ Baker, Anthony Luk**

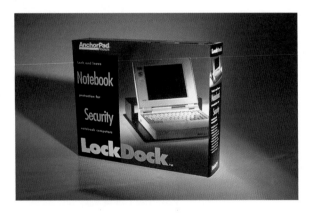

Client: **Ivie Industries**
Design Firm: **Rieches Baird**
Designer: **Susan Campbell**

Client: **Nestlé Beverage Company—Sarks**
Design Firm: **Primo Angeli, Inc.**
Designers: **Terrence Tong, Brody Hartman, Paul Terrill, Primo Angeli, Rolando Rosles**

Client: **Nestlé Beverage Company—Coffee-mate Liquid**
Design Firm: **Primo Angeli, Inc.**
Designers: **Terrence Tong, Jan Layman, Primo Angeli, Rolando Rosles**

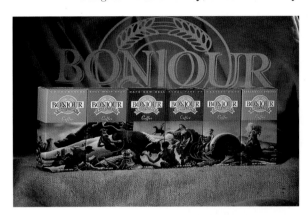

Client: **Cafe Vienna**
Design Firm: **Minneapolis Design Company**
Designer: **Robert Warren Carlson**

Client: **Caffé Roma Coffee Roasting Co.**
Design Firm: **Cahan & Associates**
Designer: **Kevin Roberson**

Client: **Starbucks Coffee Company—Mazagran**
Design Firm: **Hornall Anderson Design Works, Inc.**
Designers: **Jack Anderson, Julie Lock, Julie Keenan, Suzanne Haddon**

105

Client: **Screen Printing Supplies**
Design Firm: **Minneapolis Design Company**
Designer: **Robert Warren Carlson**

Client: **Centigram Communications Corp.**
Design Firm: **Brad Terres Design**
Designer: **Brad Terres**

Client: **Light Source**
Design Firm: **Monnens-Addis Design**
Designers: **Rick Atwood, David Rich, David Leong, Tin Chu, Joel Glenn**

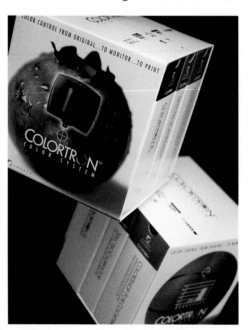

Client: **Intek Technologies**
Design Firm: **Young & Martin Design**
Designers: **Ed Young, Steve Martin**

106

Client: **Young Presidents' Organization**
New Member Kit
Design Firm: **Swieter Design United States**
Designer: **John Swieter**

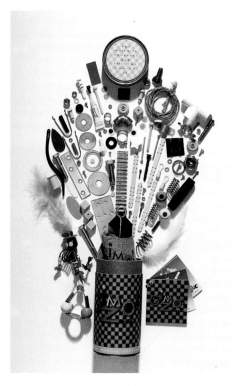

Client: **Vaughn Wedeen Creative—GIZMO**
Design Firm: **Vaughn Wedeen Creative, Inc.**
Designer: **Rick Vaughn**

Client: **Found Stuff Paper Works**
Design Firm: **Mires Design**
Designers: **Tracy Sabin,**
José Serrano

Client: **EDS Leadership Development**
Design Firm: **EDS Marketing Communications**
Designers: **Gary Daniels, Linda Bleck**

Client: **Kraft Foods, Inc.—Jell-O**
Design Firm: **Hughes Design**
Designers: **Hughes Design**

Client: **The Pillsbury Company**
Design Firm: **Hillis Mackey & Company**
Designer: **Randy Szarzynski**

Client: **Dandy Gum**
Design Firm: **The Madison Group**
Designers: **Brian Flahive, Dana Miller**

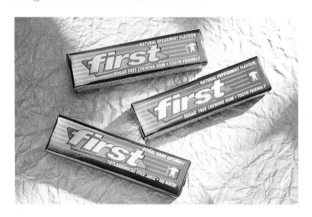

Client: **Nonni's—Cafe Biscotti**
Design Firm: **Bruce Yelaska Design**
Designer: **Bruce Yelaska**

Client: **Dean Foods Company**
Design Firm: **Hillis Mackey & Company**
Designer: **Terri Gray**

Client: **Keebler Company—Chip Chasers**
Design Firm: **Harbauer/Bruce Design, Ltd.**
Designers: **Steve Walker, Annette Ohlsen**

108

Client: **Nissan Foods (USA) Co., Inc.**
Design Firm: **Shimokochi/Reeves**
Designers: **Mamoru Shimokochi, Anne Reeves**

Client: **Astor Chocolate Corp.**
Hollywood Chocolates
Design Firm: **Maddocks & Co.**
Designers: **Julia Precht, Stephanie Valchar**

Client: **Joseph Schmidt Confections—Spring Truffles**
Design Firm: **Mühlhäuser & Young**
Designers: **Barbara Mülhäuser, Bonnie Matza**

Client: **Jimmie's Foods, Inc.**
Design Firm: **Profile Design**
Designers: **Kenichi Nishiwaki, Anthony Luk**

Client: **Metropolis Fine Confections**
Design Firm: **The Design Company**
Designers: **Fran McKay, Marcia Romanuck**

Client: **Nestlé Foods—Nestlé Nips**
Design Firm: **Primo Angeli, Inc.**
Designers: **Jenny Baker, Paul Terrill,**
Darryl Reed, Primo Angeli, Carlo Pagoda

Client: **Plantation Peanuts of Wakefield**
Design Firm: **Smith & Hall**
Designers: **Dann Hall, Christina Toler**

Client: **Snack Factory Product Line**
Design Firm: **Bailey Design Group**
Designer: **Steve Perry**

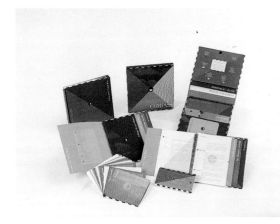

Client: **PREPCO**
Design Firm: **In house**
Designer: **Carole Pixler**

Client: **Lifelines—Compass**
Design Firm: **1185 Design**
Designer: **Julia Foug, Peggy Burke**

Letterheads

Client: **Adtech**
Design Firm: **O'Keefe Marketing**
Designer: **Jeff Schaich**

Client: **Brave Hearts**
Design Firm: **BauMac Communications**
Designer: **Tara Baumann**

Client: **Corporate Environments**
Design Firm: **Mayer/Reed**
Designers: **Michael Reed, Christina Laliberté,
Glen Marcusen**

CORPORATE ENVIRONMENTS

Client: **Arts 220**
Design Firm: **Group Chicago**
Designer: **Barbara Lynk**

MARK E. JONES, CPA

Client: **Culinary Arts & Entertainment**
Design Firm: **After Hours Creative**
Designers: **After Hours Creative**

culinary arts & entertainment

Client: **Mark E. Jones, CPA**
Design Firm: **Michael J. O'Keefe & Associates**
Designers: **Michael J. O'Keefe, Tim Watson**

7610 e. mcdonald dr. suite b. scottsdale, az 85250
tel: 602 990 5810 tel: 800 211 5844 fax: 602 990 9064

Client: **Designhaus**
Design Firm: **Widmeyer Design**
Designer: **Dale Hart**

Client: **Helix**
Design Firm: **Helix**
Designers: **Gordon Doucette, Michael Muncy**

aerea

Client: **University Eye**
Design Firm: **McElveney & Palozzi Design Group**
Designer: **Jonathan Westfall**

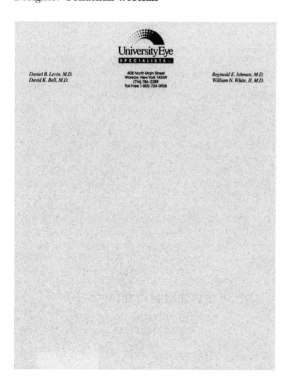

Client: **Aerea**
Design Firm: **Lawrence Design Group, Inc.**
Designer: **Marie-Christine Lawrence**

113

Client: **Caffe A Go-Go**
Design Firm: **The Rittenhouse Group, Inc.**
Designer: **Shelby Keefe**

Client: **Quick Quality Press**
Design Firm: **JCnB Design**
Designer: **Jane Nass Barnidge**

QUICK QUALITY PRESS 334 West Mifflin Street, Madison, WI 53703 608 251 7300 Fax 608 251 2141

Client: **Easy Data Systems**
Design Firm: **Turner Design**
Designer: **Bert Turner**

Client: **Keynote Arts Associates**
Design Firm: **VR Design**
Designer: **Victor Rodriguez**

KEYNOTE ARTS ASSOCIATES, INC.

MUSICIANS WORKING for MUSICIANS

Client: **US West In-Sync**
Design Firm: **Vaughn Wedeen Creative, Inc.**

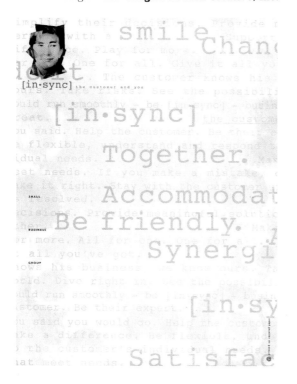

Client: **BBN Planet**
Design Firm: **Barrett Communications, Inc.**
Designer: **Nadine Flowers**

Client: **Vail Associates, Inc.**
Design Firm: **Communications Arts, Inc.**
Designers: **Lynn Williams, Henry Beer**

 GAME CREEK CLUB

Client: **Campaign for the Sisters of Mercy
and Trocaire College**
Design Firm: **Crowley Webb + Associates**
Designer: **Dion Pender**

Client: **Valley Oral & Maxillofacial Surgery**
Design Firm: **Anderson Mraz Design**
Designers: **John Mraz, Sherwin Schwartzrock**

Seven J.F.K. Street • Harvard Square • Cambridge, Massachusetts 02138 • (617) 661-3676 • FAX (617) 354-1984

Client: **Vision House**
Design Firm: **Z Design**
Designer: **Shahen Zarookian**

ARTISTS AND MUSIC   ESTABLISHED 1962

A & M RECORDS INC.
1416 NORTH LA BREA AVENUE
HOLLYWOOD, CALIFORNIA 90028
TELEPHONE 213/469-2411 FAX 213/856-2800

Client: **Winter Architects**
Design Firm: **401**
Designer: **Dana Britton**

Client: **A&M Records**
Designer: **Jeri Heiden**

Client: **Foster Film, Inc.**
Design Firm: **The Prime Time Group**
Designer: **Ted Burn**

Foster Film, Inc.

Barry Foster,

Director

608 Anniston Ave.

Gulfport,

Mississippi

39507

(601) 896-1989

P.O. BOX 5301, BELLA VISTA, AR 72714-0301 (501) 855-9328

Client: **Bella Vista Townhouse Association**
Design Firm: **Gregory Group, Inc.**
Designers: **Jon Gregory, Gary Willmann**

Client: **Jones Murphy, Inc.**
Design Firm: **Visually Speaking, Ltd.**
Designer: **Craig P. Kirby**

15 East Main Street · Richmond, Virginia 23219
804-788-8023 · Fax 788-8029

Client: **Gabbert & Hood Photography**
Design Firm: **O'Keefe Marketing**
Designer: **David King**

6711 OLD STONEHOUSE LANE · NEW MARKET, MARYLAND 21774 · PHONE 301·831·3234

117

Smyth Companies
1085 Snelling Avenue North
Saint Paul, Minnesota 55108
T 612.646.4544
F 612.646.8947
800.642.4544

Client: **Brattle Courier Service**
Design Firm: **Communication Via Design**
Designer: **Victoria Adjami**

Client: **Smyth Companies**
Design Firm: **LEC Limited**

TEL 617.547.7800
FAX 617.661.7310

76 Hampshire Street Cambridge, Massachusetts 02139

MONARCH
PICTURES

Client: **Grinnell Campaign, Grinnell College**
Design Firm: **Design Ranch**
Designers: **Gary Gnade, Chris Gnade, Danette Angerer**

GRINNELL
CAMPAIGN

Grinnell College
Office of Development
and Alumni Relations
P.O. Box 805
Grinnell, Iowa 50112-0806
515.269.3300
515.269.3322 fax

9350 W. Washington Blvd.
David Lean Building, Suite 430
Culver City, CA. 90232

T 310.280.7555
F 310.280.4959

Client: **Monarch Pictures**
Design Firm: **Gregory Thomas Associates**
Designer: **Gregory Thomas**

Building for an even brighter future

Client: **Eisenman Anderson**
Design Firm: **Yamamoto Moss**
Designers: **Hideki Yamamoto, Christy Nesja**

E I S E N M A N
A N D E R S O N

The Art of Designing Public Spaces
7001 University Avenue Southeast, Minneapolis MN 55414 Phone 612 623 1800 Fax 612 623 0012

Client: **Alcorn & Associates**
Design Firm: **Duncan/Day Advertising**
Designers: **Stacey Day, Leslie Duncan**

2717 Holly Brook Court • Bedford, Texas • 76021 • Metro 817/858 0544 • Fax 817/545-0969

Client: **Linda Wedeen**
Design Firm: **Vaughn Wedeen Creative, Inc.**
Designer: **Steve Wedeen**

W

a

Client: **PERK'S**
Design Firm: **Badertscher Communications**
Designers: **Steve Badertscher,
Dick Moulton, Cheri Nauman**

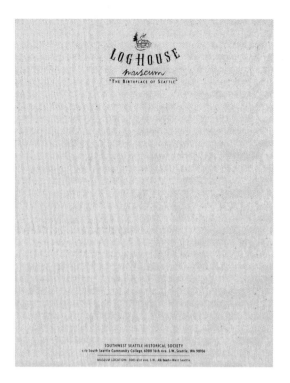

Client: **Southwest Seattle Historical Society**
Design Firm: **Gable Design Group**
Designers: **Tony Gable, Rosemary Woods,**
Wilhelmina Palance

Client: **Rochioli Vineyard & Winery**
Design Firm: **Buttitta Design**
Designers: **Patti Buttitta, Lisa Hobro**

Client: **Rock and Roll Hall of Fame + Museum**
Design Firm: **Nesnadny + Schwartz**
Designers: **Mark Schwartz, Joyce Nesnadny,**
Michelle Moehler

CHERYL S. CITRON, M.D., F.A.A.D.
Dermatology & Dermatologic Surgery

Diplomate, American Board of Dermatology
Fellow, American Academy of Dermatology

Client: **Cheryl S. Citron, M.D., F.A.A.D.**
Design Firm: **Graphics 2**
Designers: **Molly Feeney, Kathy Feeney,**
Colleen Feeney

Client: **Snowden & Roy**
Design Firm: **Adkins/Balchunas**
Designers: **Jerry Balchunas, Carol Adkins**

SNOWDEN & ROY

FINE
IMPORTED
LINENS
ANTIQUES

51 ROYAL PALM PLAZA, 300 ESPLANADE
BOCA RATON, FLORIDA 33432
PHONE: 407-392-4414 FAX: 407-392-0441

Ingrid
The Source for Creative Professionals

6947 Coal Creek Parkway S E #1200
Newcastle, WA 98059-3159
206.603.1833   FAX 206.747.8991

Client: **Ingrid Carruthers**
Design Firm: **Walsh and Associates, Inc.**
Designer: **Michael Stearns**

Client: **Pahnke Charney Chiropractic & Back Rehab**
Design Firm: **Harrisberger Creative**
Designer: **Lynn Harrisberger**

PAHNKE CHARNEY
CHIROPRACTIC & BACK REHAB

PLANET 1

COMSAT Mobile Communications
6560 Rock Spring Drive
Bethesda, Maryland 20817
Phone 301.214.3000
Fax 301.214.7100

751 THIMBLE SHOALS BLVD.
NEWPORT NEWS
VIRGINIA 23606
PHONE: 804-873-3225
FAX: 804-873-2251

Client: **COMSAT, Planet 1**
Design Firm: **HC Design**
Designers: **Howard Clare, Chuck Sundin**

121

Xplor Media Group   Tel. 619 541 8200
2721 Conway Court   Fax 619 541 8211
San Diego, CA 92111   xplor@evolve.com

Client: **MIDCOM**
Design Firm: **Hornall Anderson Design Works, Inc.**
Designers: **John Hornall, Jana Nishi, David Bates**

MIDCOM

Client: **Xplor Media Group**
Design Firm: **In House**
Designer: **Jane Higgins**

Sugar Plums

The Unique Child Development Center

Client: **Lin/Weinberg**
Design Firm: **Carnase, Inc.**
Designer: **Tom Carnase**

WEINBERG

20TH CENTURY DESIGN

84 WOOSTER STREET
NEW YORK, NY 10012
TEL. 212 219 3022
FAX. 212 219 1034

Client: **Sugar Plums Child Development Center**
Design Firm: **Barbieri & Green, Inc.**
Designers: **Adriana Barbieri, Barbara Green,
   Buddy Vagnoni**

Client: **Odessa Design**
Design Firm: **AGdesign**
Designer: **Amanda Grupe**

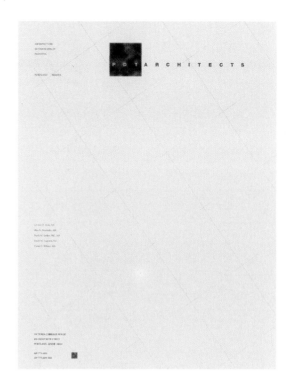

Client: **PDT Architects**
Design Firm: **Thibault Paolini Design Associates**
Designer: **Judith Paolini**

Client: **Metropolitan Ballroom & Clubroom**
Design Firm: **Little & Company**
Designers: **Tom Riddle, Jim Jackson**

Client: **Aspen Ridge Holdings**
Design Firm: **Forrest & Associates**
Designer: **Sheri F. Hammonds**

Client: **Ballets de San Juan**
Design Firm: **Graf, Inc.**
Designer: **Irma Sanabria**

BALLETS DE SAN JUAN

Tel/Fax 809 725 9140   PO Box 5 5713   San Juan PR 00901

Client: **New Orleans Fun & Games**
Design Firm: **Degnen Associates, Inc.**
Designers: **Stephen Degnen,**
David Fowler, Neil Motts

MONTAGE
NEW MEDIA TEAMS AND TALENT

520 Pike Street

Suite 1310

Seattle, WA 98101

TEL 206.623.7800

FAX 206.623.7866

Client: **Montage**
Design Firm: **Team Design, Inc.**
Designers: **David Hastings, Karla Chin**

Client: **Kollig Furniture Studio**
Design Firm: **VR Design**
Designer: **Victor Rodriguez**

Kollig Furniture Studio, Inc.
6900 Oak Highland / Kalamazoo, Michigan 49009
Shop 616 372 0647 / Office & Showroom 616 375 1645
By appointment

KOLLIG
furniture studio, inc.

124

Client: **Offshore Concepts**
Design Firm: **Basler Design Group**
Designer: **Bill Basler**

701 WEST 2ND • P.O. BOX 338 • FERRYSBURG • MICHIGAN • 49409

UNIVERSITY
LANGUAGE
CENTER

COMPLETE
TRANSLATING &
INTERPRETING
SERVICES

1313 Fifth Street S.E., Suite 201, Minneapolis, MN 55414 USA
612-379-3825 or 800-788-0032 fax 612-379-3832 e-mail 72113.3550@compuserve.com
Member American Translators Association

Client: **University Language Center**
Design Firm: **Peggy Lauritsen Design Group**
Designer: **Michelle Solie**

Client: **Nextlink**
Design Firm: **Hornall Anderson Design Works, Inc.**
Designers: **Jack Anderson, Mary Hermes, John Anicker,
Mary Chin Hutchison, Larry Anderson, David Bates**

NEXTLINK

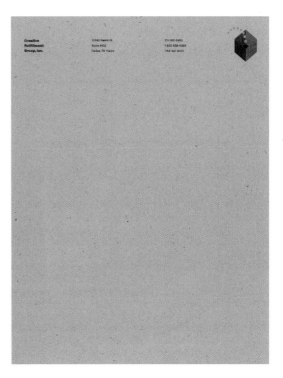

Client: **Creative Fulfillment Group**
Design Firm: **Nexus, A Design Group, Inc.**
Designer: **Shannon DeCraene**

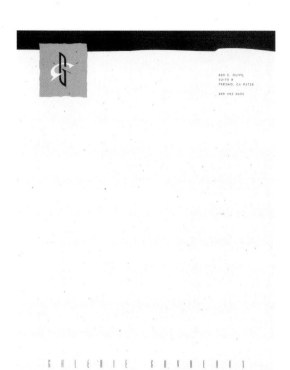

609 E. OLIVE
SUITE B
FRESNO, CA 93728

209 445 0695

G A L E R I E   G O V R E A U X

Client: **Galerie Govreaux**
Design Firm: **Parola Design**
Designers: **Jeff Barkema, Michael Parola**

Client: **Jones Intercable—Futurecom**
Design Firm: **Vaughn Wedeen Creative, Inc.**

The future of telecommunications never looked so good.

FUTURECOM

Jones Intercable, Inc.

617-A South Pickett Street

Alexandria, VA 22304

(703) 823-3000

Fax: (703) 823-3061

Community Foundation
of Central Florida, Inc.

P.O. Box 2971

Orlando, Florida

32802

(407) 872-3000

Board of Directors

Louis T. M. Conti, Esquire
Gerald F. Hilbrich, CPA
James A. Shuster
Theodore J. Burgoyne
Frank M. Hubbard
Richard T. Hoyt, Esquire
H. Clifford Lee
John S. Lord
The Honorable Alex J. Reddick
Joan Ruffier
Holly Stuart
Jo Overstreet Thacker, Esquire
Marshall E. Vermillion
Robert E. Waggoner
Royce R. Walden
Thomas G. Yochum

Executive Director
William C. Schwartz
President
Richard T. Hoyt
Vice-President
Louis T. M. Conti
Secretary
Beverly J. Pecek, CFP
Treasurer
George F. Maynard III

Client: **Scott Hull Associates**
Designer: **Al Hidalgo**

SCOTT
HULL
ASSOC
INC

68 EAST FRANKLIN ST.
DAYTON, OHIO
4 5 4 5 9

Client: **Community Foundation of Central Florida, Inc.**
Design Firm: **Magic Pencil Studios**
Designer: **Scott Feldmann**

126

Client: **Proformance Sports Marketing**
Design Firm: **Swieter Design United States**
Designers: **John Swieter, Paul Munsterman**

PRO@
FORMANCE

Sports Marketing
16816 Dallas Parkway
Suite 2400
Dallas, Texas 75248
217-733-1785
fax 214-733-3119

Client: **ProAmerica**
Design Firm: **Blanchard Schaefer Advertising**
Designers: **Mari Madison,
Jan Blanchard, Kathy Wolf**

AD CLUB

Client: **Monarch Aviation Services, Inc.**
Design Firm: **Steve Horvath Design, Inc.**
Designer: **Steve Horvath**

2750 North Frederick Avenue
Milwaukee, WI 53211-3631
voice/fax 414 964 0557
cellular 414 861 6419

monarch
AVIATION SERVICES, INC.

Client: **Ad Club—
Advertising Federation of Greater Hampton Roads**
Design Firm: **Harrisberger Creative**
Designer: **Lynn Harrisberger**

127

1748 Delmar Place • Atlanta, Georgia 30318 • tv 404. 351. 6776 • tv 404. 350. 4549

Client: **The Cook Editions, Ltd.**
Design Firm: **Rousso + Associates**
Designer: **Steve Rousso**

Client: **COW**
Design Firm: **COW**

Client: **COW**
Design Firm: **COW**

310 264 2424   310 264 2430
TELEPHONE   FACSIMILE
cow. i572-e cloverfield boulevard santa monica california 90404 3522

SUZANNE TICK

636 Broadway, Suite 504, New York, NY 10012   Telephone: 212.596.9611 Telefax: 212.596.1031

Client: **Suzanne Tick**
Design Firm: **Copeland Hirthler design + communications**
Designers: **Brad Copeland, Sean Goss**

Client: **Ripplesteins**
Design Firm: **Vaughn Wedeen Creative, Inc.**

128

Client: **The Finishing Touch**
Design Firm: **Sayles Graphic Design**
Designer: **John Sayles**

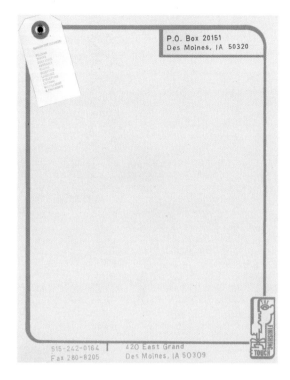

Client: **The Lookinglass Company**
Design Firm: **Arias Associates**
Designers: **Mauricio Arias, Karin Bryant**

Client: **Society for the Revival & Preservation**
   of Southern Food
Design Firm: **Rousso & Associates**
Designer: **Steve Rousso**

Client: **Designhaus International**
Design Firm: **Suissa Design**
Designer: **Joel Suissa**

SEMAPHORE

Semaphore, Inc
3 East 28th Street
New York, NY 10016
212 543 7800
212 543 7443 Fax

Semaphore West
747 South Lemon Avenue
Walnut, CA 91789
909 398 7293
909 595 1883 Fax

Client: **American Library Association**
Design Firm: **Pressley Jacobs Design**
Designer: **Jamie Gannon**

Client: **Semaphore**
Design Firm: **Lee + Yin**
Designer: **Chris Yin**

ICONIX
INC

Client: **Bruggeman Design Group**
Design Firm: **Basler Design Group**
Designer: **Bill Basler**

Client: **Iconix, Inc.**
Design Firm: **Iconix, Inc.**
Designer: **Kelly J. Schwartz**

130

Client: **Brett Callero Design**
Design Firm: **Brett Callero Design**
Designer: **Brett Callero**

Keller Groves, Inc.

HERMAN J. KELLER, President / P.O. BOX 7369, HAINES CITY, FLORIDA 33872 / PHONE 813.772.5801

Client: **Keller Groves**
Design Firm: **JOED Design**
Designer: **Ed Rebek**

GOLDEN GATE PARK CONSERVANCY

Client: DiSanto Design
Design Firm: **DiSanto Design**
Designer: **Roseanne DiSanto**

DISANTO DESIGN
TWO MELROSE ST #2
BOSTON, MA 02116
617.266.9006

A public/private
partnership of
Friends of Recreation
& Parks

McLaren Lodge • Golden Gate Park • San Francisco • CA 94117 • 415 751 1809 • F (415) 221 1993

Client: **Friends of Recreation and Parks**
Design Firm: **Bobby Reich-Parti Grafix**
Designer: **Bobby Reich-Patri**

131

ec⊙mat

Client: **Island Cowboy Unlimited**
Design Firm: **Gregory Group, Inc.**
Designer: **Jon Gregory**

Client: **Ecofranchising, Inc.**
Design Firm: **Stephen Loges Graphic Design**
Designer: **Stephen Loges**

HERSETH FRIEDMAN
& associates

Client: **Apple Valley International, Inc.**
Design Firm: **Berni Design**
Designer: **Jung Kim**

OLD ORCHARD

APPLE VALLEY INTERNATIONAL, INC.

STRATEGIC PLANNING • CREATIVE DEVELOPMENT • MEDIA SERVICES
4309 S. Louise Ave., Suite 100, Sioux Falls, SD 57106   Phone (605) 362-9000 FAX (605) 362-9242

Client: **Herseth Friedman & Associates**
Design Firm: **Herseth Friedman & Associates**

1991 Twelve Mile Road P.O. Box 66 Sparta, MI 49345 (616) 887-1745 Fax (616) 887-6210

132

Client: **Dimensional Decking & Patio**
Design Firm: **Polloni Design**
Designer: **Alberto Polloni**

One Church.
One Child.
An African-American tradition.

LUCAS COUNTY
CHILDREN SERVICES

705 ADAMS STREET

TOLEDO, OHIO 43624

(419) 327-0606

FAX (419) 327-3082

Dimensional Decking & Patio • 11417 Creedmoor Rd. Raleigh, NC 26714 • F(919) 676-7226 • T(919) 848-9165

ENDORSED BY THE
INTERDENOMINATIONAL
MINISTERIAL ALLIANCE

Client: **Lucas County Children Services**
Design Firm: **Orwig Communications**
Designers: **Ken Orwig, Julia Orwig**

Client: **JKS Architects/Sienna Architecture Company**
Design Firm: **Design Partnership/Portland**
Designers: **K. Ambrosini, D. Rood, P. Mort, A. Koenig**

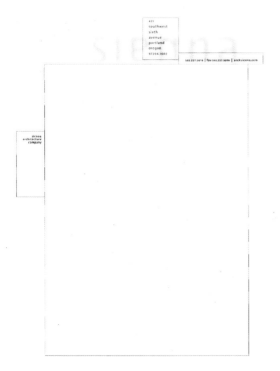

Client: **O'Keefe Marketing**
Design Firm: **O'Keefe Marketing**
Designers: **Jeff Schaich, Dave King**

DAVID SPECKMAN, PHOTOGRAPHER, 5976 BUNKER HILL RD, WILLIAMSBURG, MI 49690 TEL: 616-938-9638

Client: **David Speckman Nature Photography**
Design Firm: **Young Design**
Designer: **Peter Young**

Client: **Oasis, Inc.**
Design Firm: **Pink Coyote Design, Inc.**
Designer: **Joel Ponzan**

OASIS

Open Architecture Systems Integration Solutions, Inc.

50 Broad Street, New York, NY 10004 • Telephone: 212 843 2350 • Fax: 212 843 2355 • Oasis@oasis-inc.com

AMERICAN
TRADE &
INVESTMENT
COMPANY

Client: **Denison & Denison**
Design Firm: **VWA Group, Inc.**
Designer: **Ashley Barrow**

DENISON
&
DENISON
INTERIORS

Client: **American Trade & Investment**
Design Firm: **Design for Marketing**
Designer: **Bob Rankin**

DENISON & DENISON INTERIORS, INC.

134

Client: **Lamar Snowboards**
Design Firm: **Talbot Design Group**
Designers: **Chris Kosman, GayLyn Talbot**

Gerner and Associates, Inc.

Client: **Gerner & Associates, Inc.**
Design Firm: **Blanchard Schaefer Advertising**
Designers: **Mari Madison, Jan Blanchard**

Client: **Smith Gardens**
Design Firm: **Wright, Hart & Mather**
Designers: **Charlotte Hart, Tim Cathersal,
Toni Sims, Cale Burr**

SmithGardens
"Our Business Is Growing"

ENiD
THERAPY CENTER
Physical Therapy & Hand Rehabilitation

Client: **Enid Therapy Center**
Design Firm: **DesignForce Associates**
Designer: **Adam Nisenson**

Harry Smith Gardens, Inc. 1265 Marine Drive Bellingham, WA 98225 360-733-4671 FAX 360-647-1468

135

Telecel International Limited
Corporate: 36 Grove Street, PO Box 875, New Canaan, CT 06840 U.S.A.
Telephone: (203) 966 8623 Facsimile: (203) 966 7477

Technical: 13825 Water Pond Court, Centreville, VA 22020 U.S.A.
Telephone: (703) 631 3393 Facsimile: (703) 266 2693

Telecel

Client: **Windlight Studios, Inc.**
Design Firm: **Pat Carney Studio**
Designer: **Pat Carney**

WINDLIGHT STUDIOS, INC.

708 North First Street • Suite CR100 • Minneapolis, MN 55401
PHONE 612-359-9091 FAX 612-359-8991

Client: **Telecel**
Design Firm: **King Casey, Inc.**
Designer: **John Chrzanowski**

hands on
greenville

Client: **Oktibbeha County Economic
Development Authority**
Design Firm: **NewIdeas**
Designer: **Patty Seger**

Oktibbeha County Economic Development Authority

post office box 25696

greenville, south carolina

29616-2696

telephone 803/242-4224

Client: **Hands on Greenville**
Design Firm: **Westhouse Design**
Designers: **Jack DelGado, Daniel Jones**

136

Client: **Gametek**
Design Firm: **Hadtke Design**
Designer: **R. Karsten**

1118 Fleming Street • Key West, Florida 33040
(305) 293-9919 • (800) 654-9919 • FAX (305) 296-0357

Client: **Alexander's Guesthouse**
Design Firm: **Landmark Enterprises, Inc.**
Designer: **Shelby Keefe**

Gametek, Inc. 2999 Northeast 191st Street, Suite 500, North Miami Beach, Florida 33180 U.S.A.

Client: **Sandvik & Associates**
Design Firm: **The Design Company**
Designers: **Joel B. Freese, Mary Beth Zupec**

Colorado Asphalt Pavement Association
6880 South Yosemite Court, Suite 110
Englewood, Colorado 80112
303.741.6150 Fax 303.741.6146

Client: **Colorado Asphalt Pavement Association**
Design Firm: **Unit One, Inc.**
Designers: **Unit One, Inc.**

435 West 58th Place · Hinsdale, Illinois 60521 · Tel. 708.655.1481 · Fax 708.655.1461

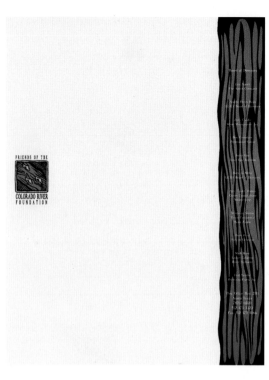

Client: **Lower Colorado River Authority**
Design Firm: **Tocquigny Advertising and Design**
Designers: **Kelley Cain, David Martino**

Client: **Global Network Services**
Design Firm: **Design Matters, Inc.**
Designers: **Gary Taylor, Andrea Taylor**

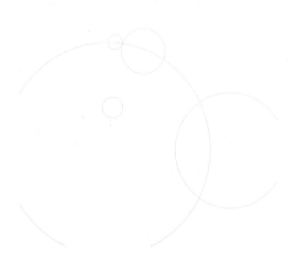

Client: **California Ostrich Co-op**
Design Firm: **Pandora & Company**
Designers: **Cathi Gunderson,
Pandora Nash-Karner, Kathy Richardson**

Client: **Spin Cycle—coin laundry**
Design Firm: **McNerney Design, Inc.**
Designers: **Sarah McNerney**

138

BACK ON TRACK
M A R K E T I N G

Client: **ImagiNet**
Design Firm: **Huntington Advertising**
Designer: **Aimee Babcock**

1677 Azusa Avenue
Suite 225
Hacienda Heights, CA 91745
Tel./Fax 818 912-1850

Client: **Back on Track Marketing**
Design Firm: **Vince Rini Design**
Designer: **Vince Rini**

4200 Commerce Court, Suite 102
Lisle, IL 60532
Phone: (708) 505-4335
Fax: (708) 505-4725
e-mail: info@imaginetbiz.com
http://www.imaginetbiz.com

VOLAN DESIGN

Volan Design LLC
1900 16th Street, Suite 101, Boulder, Colorado 80301-2822
Tel. 303-449-3838 Fax: 303-449-3128

Client: **Custom Homes by Murry**
Design Firm: **Heartland Advertising**
Designer: **Scott Stuber**

CUSTOM HOMES
BY MURRY
SINCE 1928

Client: **Volan Design LLC**
Design Firm: **Volan Design LLC**
Designer: **Michele Braverman**

1899 Lititz Pike • Lancaster, PA 17601 • (717) 569-0495 • Fax (717) 560-0391

139

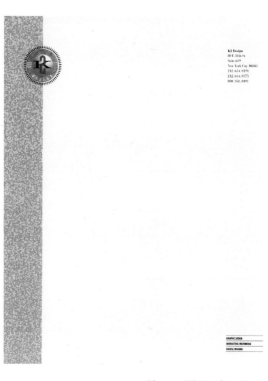

Client: **MOTIF**
Design Firm: **Group Chicago**
Designer: **Kurt Meinecke**

Client: **K2 Design, Inc.**
Design Firm: **K2 Design, Inc.**
Designers: **Douglas Cleek, Brad Szollose**

Client: **Excell Models + Phototyping**
Design Firm: **Polivka Logan Design**
Designer: **Chris Adams**

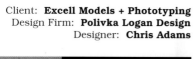

Client: **Alexa Stirling, L.P.**
Design Firm: **Silver Communications, Inc.**
Designers: **Gregg Sibert, Sally Hiesiger**

Client: **Landau & Heyman**
Design Firm: **Gibson Communication Group, Inc.**
Designer: **Chuck Snider**

M A E S T R O 🌑 Marketing and Public Relations
5015 Lassen Avenue
San Jose, CA 95129-4909
ph: 408-996-9975
fx: 408-996-8531

Client: **Barbara S. Kalkis**
Design Firm: **Ideas for Advertising & Design**
Designer: **Noel Voskuil**

Client: **Rolling Cones**
Design Firm: **Widmeyer Design**
Designers: **Dale Hart, Ken Widmeyer, Tony Secolo**

7134 Countrywood Lane
Madison Wisconsin 53719

voice 608-695-9283
page 608-559-9399
fax 608-845-8451

Client: **Image Gate**
Design Firm: **Z•D Studios, Inc.**
Designers: **Mark Schmitz, Chris Maddox**

ROLLING CONES, INC. 117 E. LOUISA STREET SUITE # 315 SEATTLE, WA 98102 PHONE 206.527.0380 ☏

141

Client: **Boelts Brothers Associates**
Design Firm: **Boelts Brothers Associates**
Designers: **Eric Boelts, Jackson Boelts,
Kerry Stratford**

Client: **Iconix**
Design Firm: **Iconix**
Designers: **Sidney Barcelona, Ted Smith**

Client: **NBBJ Sports and Entertainment**
Design Firm: **NBBJ Graphic Design**
Designer: **Dan Smith**

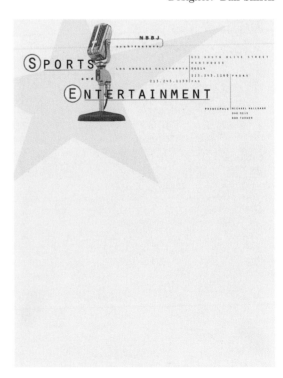

Client: **Jones Murphy, Inc.**
Design Firm: **Visually Speaking, Ltd.**
Designer: **Craig P. Kirby**

142

Client: **Creatures of Habit**
Design Firm: **Gregory R. Farmer/Fire House, Inc.**
Designer: **Gregory R. Farmer**

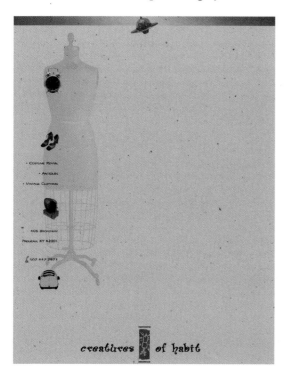

Client: **Mowbray, Inc.**
Design Firm: **Adkins/Balchunas**
Designers: **Jerry Balchunas, Carol Adkins**

Client: **Pacific Interpreters**
Design Firm: **DesignLab**
Designer: **Jim Ales**

Client: **Blooming Prairie Warehouse, Inc.**
Design Firm: **Design Ranch**
Designers: **Gary Gnade, Chris Gnade,**
Danette Angerer

143

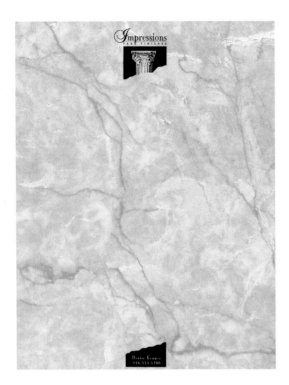

Client: **Impressions Faux Finishing**
Design Firm: **Denise Kemper Design**
Designer: **Denise Stratton Kemper**

Client: **Michael Reiff & Associates**
Design Firm: **Goldsmith/Jeffrey**
Designer: **Nora Vaivads, Dean Hacohen**

Client: **Martha Fenton**
Design Firm: **Thomas Hillman Design**
Designer: **Thomas Hillman**

Client: **Hiroshi Hamada Design Studio**
Design Firm: **Hiroshi Hamada Design Studio**
Designer: **Hiroshi Hamada**

144

Client: **Netsmith, Inc**
Design Firm: **GB Sign & Graphic**
Designers: **Alex Villa-Real, Gail Burt**

Client: **Depth of Field**
Design Firm: **Epstein, Gutzwiller, Schultz & Partners**
Designer: **John Okal**

Client: **Artisan Partners**
Design Firm: **McDill Design**
Designer: **Brad Bedessem**

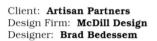

Client: **Indigo Coastal Grill**
Design Firm: **Donahue Studios, Inc.**
Designer: **Andrew Tse**

145

Client: **Radical Concepts, Inc.**
Design Firm: **Russell Leong Design**
Designer: **Russell Leong**

NYU Medical Center Food and Nutrition Service • 550 First Avenue • New York, New York 10016 • 212.263.5170

Client: **NYU Medical Center Food
and Nutrition Service**
Design Firm: **Corchia Woliner Associates**
Designer: **Todd Rhoda**

RADICAL CONCEPTS INC.

Client: **Widmeyer Design**
Design Firm: **Widmeyer Design**
Designers: **Dale Hart, Ken Widmeyer**

Client: **dot 05 Optical Communications, Inc.**
Design Firm: **Marc English: Design**
Designer: **Marc English**

146

Client: **Fresh Squeezed Design**
Design Firm: **Fresh Squeezed Design**
Designers: **Paige Keiser-Rezac, Steven Rezac**

Client: **Dairy Farmers, Inc.**
Design Firm: **Corporate Design Associates**
Designer: **Matt Taylor**

Client: **International Center for Migration,
    Ethnicity and Citizenship**
Design Firm: **DI Vision Studio**
Designers: **Cristiana Neri, Kevin Downey**

Client: **Buffalo in Bloom**
Design Firm: **Crowley Webb and Associates**
Designer: **Rob Wynne**

147

ASTRA
PHOENIX GROUP

CREATIVE INTEGRATION OF
TECHNOLOGY FOR EDUCATION

Client: **St. James sales & consulting group, ltd.**
Design Firm: **Evolution Communications**
Designer: **Pat Noonan-Hastings**

80 S. LaGrange Rd.
Suite 5
LaGrange, IL
60525
Tel. 708.784.2079
Fax. 708.784.0041

9000 W. 60TH STREET
PRAIRIE VILLAGE, KANSAS,
66207.3285

AppleLink: HARDT. R

913.383.0494
FAX 383.0954

Client: **Astra Phoenix Group**
Design Firm: **Muller + Company**
Designer: **Joann Otto**

DATA-VOICE & BEYOND ● PROVIDING TOTAL COMMUNICATIONS SOLUTIONS

GENESIS DIRECT L.L.C.

ONE BRIDGE PLAZA, SUITE 685
FORT LEE, NJ 07024-9467
201.947.8481 TEL
201.947.8426 FAX

RICHARD M. METZLER
VICE PRESIDENT
GLOBAL LOGISTICS

Client: **Taylor Subscription Talk**
Design Firm: **Striegel and Associates**
Designers: **Peggy Striegel, Tom Schmeltz,
Phill Cooper**

GENESIS
DIRECT

TST

Client: **Genesis Direct**
Design Firm: **De Plano Design**
Designers: **Vance Tritible, Gita Pabla**

TAYLOR SUBSCRIPTION TALK™
6931 S. 66th East Avenue ● Suite 110 ● Tulsa, OK ● 74133-1716 ● 1-800-789-4506 ● 1-918-481-0077 ● Fax 1-918-492-1788
MAIL: PO Box 700240 ● Tulsa, OK ● 74170-0240 ● website: http://www.tstradio.com ● email: mail@tstradio.com

Client: **Association of Farmworker**
Opportunity Programs
Design Firm: **Alphawave Designs**
Designer: **Douglas Dunbebin**

1611 North Kent Street
Suite 910
Arlington, Virginia 22209

Telephone: 703.528.4141
Fax: 703.528.4145

The National Federation of
Farmworker Training, Employment
and Service Organizations
An Equal Opportunity Employer

PRINTED ON RECYCLED PAPER

Client: **Prism Venture Partners**
Design Firm: **Tom Davis + Company**
Designers: **Way Tay, Tom Davis**

ASTRA

Astra Management Corp.

9595 Wilshire Boulevard, Suite 410
Beverly Hills, California 90212
Telephone: 310.859.9735
Facsimile: 310.285.9955

Client: **Stardock Systems**
Design Firm: **F.J. Fisher Communications, Inc.**
Designers: **Frank Fisher, Cathy Carpenter**

Stardock Systems, Inc.
7977 Ronda Drive, Suite B
Canton, Michigan 48187
Phone: 313-453-0328
Fax: 313-453-1480
Email: stardock95@aol.com.
WEB: http://aeonline.com/~stardock

Client: **Astra Management Corp.**
Design Firm: **Douglas Oliver Design Office**
Designers: **Douglas Oliver, Deanna Kuhlmann**

TEXTURES OF AFRICA
701 South Main Street, Boerne, TX 78006
ph: (210) 249-4741
fax: (210) 249-9370

Specializing in exotic leather fashions and works of art from Africa

Client: **Textures of Africa**
Design Firm: **Ledom + Pollock Advertising + Design**
Designer: **Neil Pollock**

Client: **Pitchfork Development**
Design Firm: **The Weller Institute for the
Cure of Design, Inc.**
Designer: **Don Weller**

Post Office Box 680004 Park City, Utah 84068-1004 Telephone (801)649-9979 Facsimile (801)649-9304

STORM PEAK PRESS 187 STALEY WAY SUITE 411 SEATTLE, WASHINGTON 98604 FACSIMILE 225-9044 TELEPHONE 206-225-9042

Client: **Storm Peak Press**
Design Firm: **Widmeyer Design**
Designers: **Dale Hart, Tony Secolo**

Client: **Paul Zenk**
Design Firm: **Steve Trapero Design**
Designer: **Steve Trapero**

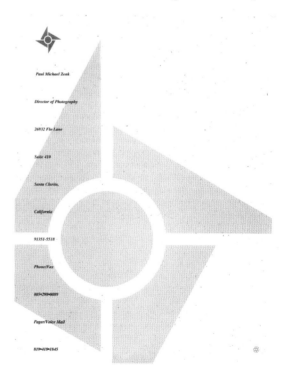

Paul Michael Zenk

Director of Photography

26932 Flo Lane

Suite 410

Santa Clarita,

California

91351-5518

Phone/Fax

805•298•0089

Pager/Voice Mail

818•419•1845

150

Client: **Die Works**
Design Firm: **Webster Design Associates**
Designers: **Dave Webster, Andrey Nagorny**

Client: **Pinnacle Enterprise**
Design Firm: **Muller + Company**
Designer: **Joann Otto**

Client: **Longwater & Co., Inc.**
Design Firm: **Longwater & Co., Inc.**
Designer: **Kitty Strozier**

Client: **The Tate Agency**
Design Firm: **The Tate Agency**
Designer: **William Cash**

151

Client: **Children's Aid & Family Services, Inc.**
Design Firm: **Words and Pictures**
Designers: **Smita Aggarwal, Angela Vairo**

Client: **Lastword Productions**
Design Firm: **Basler Design Group**
Designer: **Bill Basler**

lastword productions Cate Drew
2451 Fifth Avenue SE, Cedar Rapids, Iowa 52403
ph.319.365.4205 fx.319.365.2017 Writing, Proofing & Editing

lastword.

Client: **Advertising Design, Inc.**
Design Firm: **Advertising Design, Inc.**
Designer: **Eric Finstad**

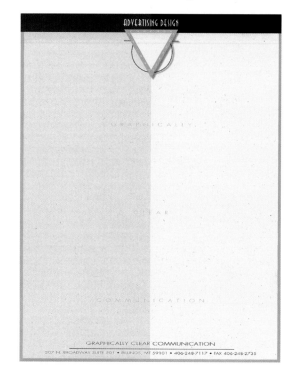

Client: **Boston Design Group**
Design Firm: **Tilka Design**
Designers: **Jane Tilka, Carla Mueller**

Client: **Rege Creative**
Designer: **Laura Medeiros**

Client: **Clientele Software**
Design Firm: **ID, Incorporated**
Designers: **Jonathan Mulcare, Dru Martin**

Client: **Moonlight Mushrooms**
Design Firm: **A to Z Communications, Inc.**
Designers: **Alan C. Boarts, Kathy Kendra**

Client: **Connolly & Connolly, Inc.**
Design Firm: **Connolly & Connolly, Inc.**
Designers: **Joseph T. Connolly, Luke Murphy**

Creekside Mushrooms Ltd.
One Moonlight Drive ❋ Worthington, PA 16262-9730 ❋ Telephone 412-297-1491 ❋ Fax 412-297-5101

Client: **Poe's Cousin**
Design Firm: **Seth Greenwald Design**
Designer: **Seth Greenwald**

901 W. Main St. | P.O. Box 842034 Richmond, VA 23284-2034 | 800 311-3341

Client: **VCU Ad Center**
Design Firm: **O'Keefe Marketing**
Designer: **Jeff Schaich**

Client: **Maurice F. Blouin, Inc.**
Design Firm: **Maurice F. Blouin, Inc.**
Designers: **Endel Koppel, Michael S. Bartley,**
Carter Wentworth

MAURICE F. BLOUIN, INC.

Client: **David Morris Design Associates**
Design Firm: **David Morris Design Associates**
Designer: **Denise M. Anderson**

Client: **DesignLab**
Design Firm: **DesignLab**
Designer: **Kennah Harcum**

DESIGNLAB
COMMUNICATIONS·SIGNAGE

P O BOX 15623   RICHMOND, VA 23227   TEL 804 264 3545   FAX 804 264 6175   Kennah@aol.com

Client: **Clifford Selbert Design**
Design Firm: **Clifford Selbert Design Collaborative**
Designer: **Darren Namaye**

the martin resource
group, inc.

479 Poplar Avenue   telephone 708-833-5995
Elmhurst, Illinois 60126   fax 708-833-3624

Client: **Ruth Weissmüller**
Design Firm: **Uschi**
Designer: **Uschi**

Ruth Weissmüller

Lichsweg 2 4310 Rheinfelden Schweiz

Tel &
061
8316665

|||

Client: **The Martin Resource Group**
Design Firm: **Pressley Jacobs Design**
Designer: **Wendy Pressley-Jacobs**

Client: **Bow Meow, Inc.**
Design Firm: **Phoenix Creative, St. Louis**
Designer: **Deborah Finkelstein**

Client: **Broom & Broom, Inc.**
Design Firm: **Broom & Broom, Inc.**
Designers: **David Broom, Deborah Hagemann**

Eagle Rehab Corporation

Client: **Intelect, Inc.**
Design Firm: **Quill Creative, Inc.**
Designer: **Steve Utley**

INTELECT, INC.

Client: **Eagle Rehab Corporation**
Design Firm: **Swieter Design United States**
Designers: **John Swieter, Mark Ford**

Client: **The Republic of Moldova**
Design Firm: **Concept Marketing Design**
Designers: **Reg Avey, Sam Marguccio**

Client: **TR Group**
Design Firm: **Group Chicago**
Designer: **Kurt Meinecke**

Client: **Cityscape Institute**
Design Firm: **Round Pond Editions**
Designers: **Juanita Dugdale, Ann Weinstock**

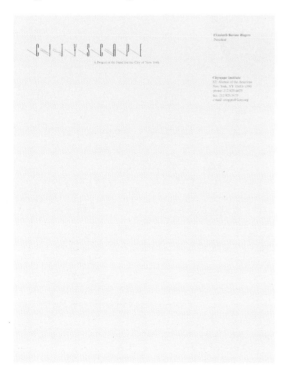

Client: **Dunnahoe Productions**
Design Firm: **Hugh Dunnahoe Illustration & Design**
Designers: **Chris Michika, Hugh Dunnahoe**

157

HOME IMPROVEMENT SPECIALISTS

J Sadler Company

J

ADDITIONS • FIREPLACES • REMODELING • KITCHENS • BATHROOMS • REPLACEMENT WINDOWS AND DOORS • DECKS

Client: **J. Sadler Company**
Design Firm: **Harrisberger Creative**
Designer: **Lynn Harrisberger**

Client: **Artisan Interactive**
Design Firm: **Roman Design**
Designer: **Lisa Romanowski**

ARTISAN INTERACTIVE

4990 SOUTH SEPULVEDA

LOS ANGELES

CALIFORNIA 90025

PHONE 310.312.3363

FAX 310.312.8657

CHICAGO • LOS ANGELES

Centennial Lakes
Dental Group

Alan Magck, D.D.S.   Centennial Lakes Medical Center
Gordon Knudson, D.D.S.   Suite 500
Steven Mahler, D.D.S.   7373 France Avenue South
Craig Freeman, D.D.S.   Edina, Minnesota 55435-4559
                          Telephone (612) 831-2900
                          Facsimile (612) 831-9805

Client: **Centennial Lakes Dental Group**
Design Firm: **Ikola designs...**
Designer: **Gale William Ikola**

TriOcean
INTERNATIONAL, LLC

Suite 1200

2000 Powell Street

Emeryville, CA 94608

Phone 510.889.6448

Fax 510.889.0065

Client: **TriOcean International, LLC**
Design Firm: **Blue Cat Studio**
Designer: **Rebecca Sobaje, Linda Zupcic**

Client: **Homedics**
Design Firm: **Zen Design Group, Ltd.**
Designer: **David Yee**

2340 Greer Blvd., Kengo Harbor, MI 46530 • Ph (810)681-9600 • Fax (810)681-1811 • Toll Free (800)333-8282

Client: **Edgewater Technology**
Design Firm: **Barrett Communications, Inc.**
Designer: **Tracy Preston**

Client: **Marshall Information Service**
Design Firm: **Pollman Marketing Arts, Inc.**
Designer: **Jennifer Pollman**

MARSHALL
INFORMATION SERVICE

Client: **Computer Systems Institute**
Design Firm: **Bullet Communications, Inc.**
Designer: **Tim Scott**

TOTO 1155 southern road, morrow, georgia 30260 united states. telephone +1 404 921 1956 facsimile +1 404 361 9645

Client: **Toto**
Design Firm: **Sagmeister**
Designer: **Stefan Sagmeister**

Client: **CRM Group**
Design Firm: **DesignForce Associates**
Designers: **Adam Nisenson, Mike Markey**

CRM GROUP

Centre for Refractive Marketing

Michael W. Malley   1407 Oxford Avenue   T. 713.880.3446
President/Founder   Studio A, Houston, Tx. 77008   F. 713.880.3466

Partners for leadership
in business and
information technology

245 East 25 Street
New York, NY 10010
212 683-7833

Vanguard
Alliance

Client: **Vanguard Alliance**
Design Firm: **Kelleher & Tait Design Group, Inc.**
Designers: **Douglas Tait, Karen Kelleher**

Client: **Health Care Imaging**
Design Firm: **perpetual designs**
Designer: **Wesley R. Porter**

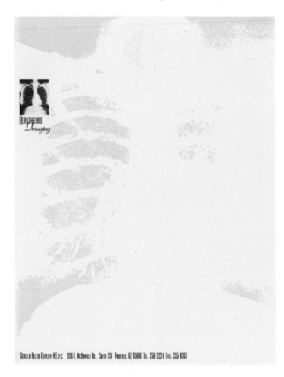

HEALTHCARE
Imaging

GEROLD ALLEN KAPLAN MD, P.C.   535 E. McDOWELL RD., SUITE 131   PHOENIX, AZ 85006   TEL. 258-2224   FAX. 255-8361

160

INTERE   RFC

Client: **Naas Chiropractic Clinic**
Design Firm: **JCnB Design**
Designer: **Jane Nass Barnidge**

Client: **Intere RFC**
Design Firm: **Douglas Oliver Design Office**
Designer: **Deanna Kuhlmann**

Client: **New Mexico Aids Walk**
Design Firm: **Vaughn Wedeen Creative, Inc.**

PJ Graphics

650 Venice Blvd.

Venice, CA 90291

Tel: 310 827-9666

Fax: 310 827-3397

Client: **Self Promotion**
Design Firm: **PJ Graphics**
Designers: **Paula Menchen, Justin Menchen**

It's bagel time!

Client: **Chesapeake Bagel**
Design Firm: **Kiku Obata & Company**
Designer: **Jane McNeely**

Client: **Grene Vision Group**
Design Firm: **Insight**
Designers: **Tracy Holdeman, Sherrie Holdeman**

UNIFYING OPHTHALMOLOGY AND OPTOMETRY TO BRING YOU COMPREHENSIVE AND CONVENIENT EYE CARE

connective solutions

Client: **Connective Solutions**
Design Firm: **Blanchard Schaefer Advertising**
Designer: **Jan Blanchard**

Client: **Love Packaging Group**
Design Firm: **Love Packaging Group**
Designer: **Tracy Holdeman**

Client: **Sharon Boguch**
Design Firm: **Hansen Design Company**
Designer: **Pat Hansen**

Client: **Debmar Studios**
Design Firm: **White Plus**
Designers: **Trina Nuovo, Victoria Berry**

Client: **TeamDesign, Inc.**
Design Firm: **TeamDesign, Inc.**
Designers: **Gary LaComa, Ross Hogin**

TEAMDESIGN

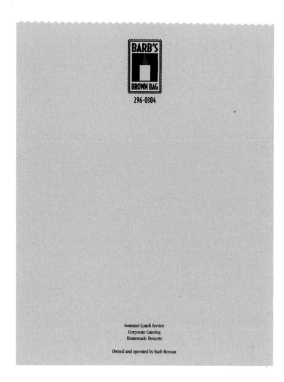

Client: **Barb's Brown Bag**
Design Firm: **Denise Kemper Design**
Designer: **Denise Stratton Kemper**

163

FLORENCE

Client: **Young Presidents' Organization,**
Florence University
Design Firm: **Swieter Design United States**
Designers: **Jenice Heo, Mark Ford**

Client: **Lominack Associates**
Design Firm: **Lominack Associates**
Designer: **Alana Swanson**

Lominack
Associates

Architects

BELYEA
DESIGN
ALLIANCE

Client: **Design Direction**
Design Firm: **Design Ranch**
Designers: **Gary Gnade, Chris Gnade,**
Danette Angerer

1906 Plaen View Drive
Iowa City, IA 52246
319.337.8572
319.337.8855 FAX

DESIGN DIRECTION

Client: **Belyea Design Alliance**
Design Firm: **Belyea Design Alliance**
Designers: **Patricia Belyea, Adrianna Jumping Eagle,**
Samantha Hunt, Jani Drewfs, Brian O'Neill

164

Client: **Barnes Geeter & Associates**
Design Firm: **VR Design**
Designers: **Victor Rodriguez, Sue Severeid**

Scott Morgan, Inc.

901
West San Mateo
Studio D
Santa Fe
New Mexico
87505

Telephone
505.986.0083

Facsimile
505.986.8971

Client: **Scott Morgan Photography**
Design Firm: **Lisa Levin Design**
Designers: **Lisa Levin, Kristy Weyhrich**

Client: **Randol Printing Services**
Design Firm: **Thom Surman Design**
Designer: **Thom Surman**

Sierra Eagle

2995 Woodside Road, Ste. 400
Woodside, CA 94062
(415) 368-1340 fax (415) 368-1341

Client: **Sierra Eagle**
Design Firm: **Gumas Communications**
Designers: **Donna Gray, David Stewart**

1804 W. Oceanfront #8.
Newport Beach,
California 92663
T 714 675-7005
E rps@randol.com
F 714 675-7365

Client: **Oh Boy, a Design Company**
Design Firm: **Oh Boy, a Design Company**
Designers: **David Salantro, Mike Kraine**

Client: **Naked Music**
Design Firm: **Sagmeister, Inc.**
Designer: **Stefan Sagmeister**

HADTKEDESIGN

Client: **CUBE Advertising/Design**
Design Firm: **CUBE Advertising/Design**
Designers: **David Chiow, Steve Wienke**

CUBE *Advertising* | *Design*

900 Broadway
New York, NY 10003
Tel 212.505.3539
Fax 212.505.9656

Client: **Hadtke Design**
Design Firm: **Hadtke Design**
Designers: **R. Karsten, F. Hadtke, R. Churchill**

Client: **Della Homenik**
Design Firm: **Point to Point**
Designer: **Karen Myers**

Client: **White Plus**
Design Firm: **White Plus**
Designers: **Trina Nuovo, Byron Lee,**
Carole Czapla, Jiyoon Jun

Client: **Stone Bridge Marketing Group**
Design Firm: **The Brochure Factory**
Designer: **Albert M. Ieronemo**

3809 GREEN TRAILS DRIVE
WOODRIDGE, IL 60517
708-355-5772
FAX 355-5773

Client: **Camp 7**
Design Firm: **Rieches Baird**
Designer: **Masa Lau**

Client: **UP Design**
Design Firm: **UP Design**
Designers: **Gary Underhill,
Wendy Peters, Carin Pombo**

María Amparo Escandón

2063 Colmar Avenue, Los Angeles, California 90039
Voice: 213/314-7790 Fax: 213/479-8043

Client: **Maria Escandon**
Design Firm: **Acento Advertising, Inc.**
Designer: **Alejandro Mayans**

Client: **Mathematical Technologies**
Design Firm: **Malcolm Grear Designers, Inc.**

Digital Restoration Services

Mathematical Technologies Inc.

One Richmond Square
Providence, RI 02906 USA
Tel 401.831.1315
Fax 401.831.1318

Client: **Clark Production Services**
Design Firm: **Pinpoint Communications**
Designers: **Dudley Davenport, Stephanie Pickett**

168

Client: **Big Dog Custom Motorcycles, Inc.**
Design Firm: **Insight**
Designers: **Tracy Holdeman, Sherrie Holdeman**

Elizabeth A. Allen, CFP
Financial Planning and
Investment Services

Client: **Elizabeth Allen, CFP**
Design Firm: **Studio Max Design, Inc.**
Designer: **Donna Wilhelm**

Client: **XactData Corporation**
Design Firm: **Hornall Anderson Design Works, Inc.**
Designers: **Jack Anderson, Lisa Cerveny,
Jana Wilson, Julie Keenan**

Client: **The Design Foundry**
Design Firm: **The Design Foundry**
Designers: **Tom Jenkins, Jane Jenkins**

169

Client: **Eagle River**
Design Firm: **John Brady Design Consultants**
Designers: **Mona MacDonald, Rick Madison,**
Sharon Bretz

Client: **Planet Comics**
Design Firm: **Kiku Obata & Company**
Designer: **Rich Nelson**

SMMA

Client: **Snelling Personnel Services**
Design Firm: **Duncan/Day Advertising**
Designer: **Stacey Day**

Client: **Symmes Maini & McKee Associates**
Design Firm: **Richard Endly Design, Inc.**
Designers: **Richard Endly, Keith Wolf, Todd Paulson**

UNITED
Correctional Managed Care, Inc.

Client: **Power Summit Communications**
Design Firm: **VR Design**
Designers: **Victor Rodriguez, Sue Severeid**

POWER
SUMMIT
COMMUNICATIONS

SUNFLOWER
STREET

BROOMFIELD
COLORADO

Video Production

Brochures

Marketing and
Strategic Planning

Newsletters

Training and
Workshops

Event Planning

Presentations

CORPORATE HEADQUARTERS:
2401 East Katella Avenue
Suite 300
Anaheim, California 92806
Tel: (714) 978-6971
Fax: (714) 978-6842
(800) 353-0320
OFFICES IN: New York and Georgia

Client: **United Correctional Managed Care**
Design Firm: **Concept 2**
Designers: **Carol Gould, Dave Belmonte**

Client: **Fitstart**
Design Firm: **Port Miolla Associates**
Designer: **Jennifer Abramson**

fit**start**
personalized well-being

The Missouri Buy Recycled Initiative   P.O. Box 744   314-526-5885 Phone
Market Development Program /DNR4   325 Jefferson Street 314-635-3406 Fax
                                        Jefferson City, Missouri
                                        65102-0744

Missouri Buys Recycled

Printed on recycled paper using soy-based inks

Client: **Missouri Buys Recycled**
Design Firm: **Kiku Obata & Company**
Designer: **Rich Nelson**

186 Milbank Avenue
Greenwich, CT 06830
phone 203.622.1793

171

Client: **The Rodeo
electronic prepress studio**
Design Firm: **Spangler Associates**
Designer: **Michael Connors**

Client: **Thorenfeldt Construction**
Design Firm: **Keng's Designs**
Designer: **Robert Keng**

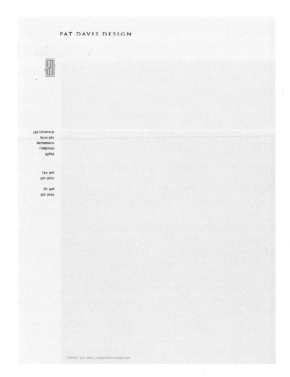

Client: **Pat Davis Design**
Design Firm: **Pat Davis Design**
Designers: **Andrea Johnston, Steve Donatelli**

Client: **Real Art Design Group, Inc.**
Design Firm: **Real Art Design Group, Inc.**
Designers: **Greg Tobias, Chris Wire**

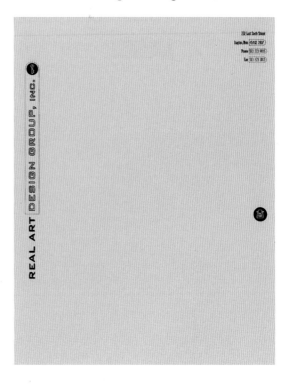

Client: **Goldforest Advertising**
Design Firm: **Goldforest Advertising**
Designer: **Sally Ann Field**

Client: **Pat Carney Studio**
Design Firm: **Pat Carney Studio**
Designer: **Lizabeth Montgomery**

Client: **Pierson Hawkins, Inc. Advertising**
Design Firm: **Pierson Hawkins, Inc. Advertising**
Designers: **Michael Besch, Janelle Aune, Chip Hisle**

Client: **Design Milwaukee**
Design Firm: **Becker Design**
Designer: **Neil Becker**

Client: **White Arts Printing**
Design Firm: **Indiana Design Consortium, Inc.**

Client: **Mormac**
Design Firm: **TAB Graphics Design, Inc.**
Designers: **TAB Graphics Design, Inc.**

Client: **Karat Interactive**
Design Firm: **Pollman Marketing Arts, Inc.**
Designers: **Jennifer Pollman, Kristen DeSantis**

Client: **Mezcal Importers, Inc.**
Design Firm: **Banks & Associates**
Designer: **Lionel Banks**

174

Client: **The Bowyer Studio**
Design Firm: **O'Keefe Marketing**
Designer: **Jeff Schaich**

Client: **Jim Walker**
Design Firm: **Steel Wool Design**
Designer: **Kristy Lewis**

Client: **Good Net**
Design Firm: **After Hours Creative**
Designers: **After Hours Creative**

Client: **Disegno**
Design Firm: **Disegno**
Designer: **Cathy Barnard**

175

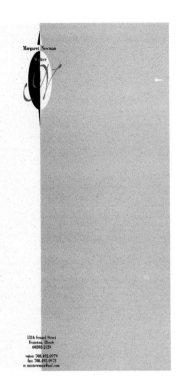

Client: **Margaret Newman**
Design Firm: **Alan Brunettin Illustration**
Designer: **Alan Brunettin**

Client: **Solutions at Work**
Design Firm: **Graphic Access Design**
Designer: **Gloria Keibler**

SOLUTIONS **AT WORK** Inc.

90 BRANDON ROAD, NORTHFIELD, ILLINOIS 60093
708-887-8892 FAX 708-887-8893

Client: **Belviso Creative Services**
Design Firm: **Belviso Creative Services**
Designers: **Bob Belviso, Steve Ong**

Client: **Philadelphia Chamber Music Society**
Design Firm: **Randi Margrabia Design**
Designer: **Randi Shalit Margrabia**

belviso creative services 230 park avenue suite 910 new york 10169
(212) 661-6775 fax 661-7393

Client: **The Marshall Companies, Inc.**
Design Firm: **Swieter Design United States**
Designer: **John Swieter**

Client: **P, G & E Enterprises/Vantus**
Design Firm: **Lisa Levin Design**
Designers: **Lisa Levin, Sam Lising**

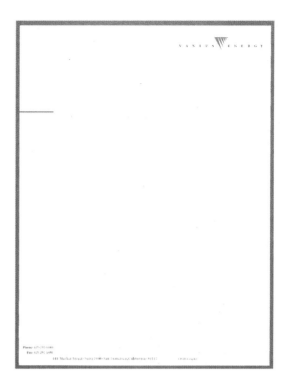

Client: **Carolyn Rodi Design Group**
Design Firm: **Carolyn Rodi Design Group**
Designer: **Carolyn Rodi**

Client: **BRD Design**
Design Firm: **BRD Design**
Designer: **Peter King Robbins**

177

Client: **Encara**
Design Firm: **Little & Company**
Designers: **Kathy Soranno, Jim Jackson**

Encara

7603 Gramercy Road Suite 101 Bloomington, MN 55437
T (612) 831-6690 (800) 595-4927 F (612) 831-7692

Client: **The Meadows of Napa Valley**
Design Firm: **BauMac Communication**
Designer: **Tara Baumann**

EN GRUPO

Client: **PLD**
Design Firm: **PLD**
Designer: **Chris Adams**

En Grupo, Inc.
1452 Condominio Asia Ligia
Suite #411 B
Condado, PR 00907
Tel./Fax 809 725 9111
Beeper 250 0160
Unidad 57864

Client: **Engrupo, Inc.**
Design Firm: **ID Group**
Designers: **Astrid Flores, Abner Gutierrez, Mayra Maldonado**

Client: **Lenox Room**
Design Firm: **Aerial**
Designer: **Tracy Moon**

Client: **Weaver Design**
Design Firm: **Weaver Design**
Designer: **Marie Weaver**

Client: **Roger Christian & Company**
Design Firm: **Roger Christian & Company**
Designer: **Roger Christian**

Client: **ID, Incorporated**
Design Firm: **ID, Incorporated**
Designers: **Jonathan Mulcare, Dru Martin**

Client: **Little & Company**
Design Firm: **Little & Company**
Designers: **Garin Ipsen, Paul Wharton**

Client: **Tracy Sabin Graphic Design**
Design Firm: **Tracy Sabin Graphic Design**
Designer: **Tracy Sabin**

Client: **Wild Honey**
Design Firm: **Wild Honey**
Designers: **Gennady Spirin, Bea Jackson**

Client: **Allan C. Jones, D.D.S.**
Design Firm: **Palko Advertising**
Designers: **Dave Kolosvary, Chuck Waldman**

Client: **NewIdeas**
Design Firm: **NewIdeas**
Designer: **Patty O. Seger**

Client: **LRS Architects**
Design Firm: **Design Partnership/Portland**
Designers: **K. Ambrosini, D. Shishkoff**

Client: **LifeNet Health Plans, HMO, Inc.**
Design Firm: **Design Services, Inc.**
Designers: **Rod Parker, Todd Palisi**

Client: **Task Group**
Design Firm: **Ford & Earl Associates, Inc.**
Designer: **Susan J. Garrett**

Client: **Andrea Clasen**
Design Firm: **Rieches Baird**
Designer: **Carrie Sandoval**

ANDREA CLASEN
ORGANIZATIONAL & OPERATIONAL CONSULTING

P.O. BOX 3312
NEWPORT BEACH, CALIFORNIA 92659
TEL 714-675-9853 FAX 714-723-5803

Annette's Drapery Designs, Inc.
4145 WEST 207TH STREET ~ MATTESON, ILLINOIS 60443 ~ 708.481.8187 PHONE/FAX

Client: **Annette's Drapery Design**
Design Firm: **Roman Design**
Designer: **Lisa Romanowski**

Barrington
Business & Engineering Solutions

B

PHOENIX
LOS ANGELES
SAN FRANCISCO
CHICAGO
NEW YORK
PITTSBURGH
DALLAS
WASHINGTON, D.C.

1114 Avenue of the Americas 30th Floor The Grace Building New York, New York 10036 Tel. 212 819-9300 Fax. 212 819-9818

Client: **Barrington Consulting Group**
Design Firm: **White Design, Inc.**
Designers: **John White, Aram Youssefian**

Client: **Antista Fairclough Design**
Design Firm: **Antista Fairclough Design**
Designers: **Tom Antista, Thomas Fairclough**

Client: **EDCO Builders**
Design Firm: **Steve Trapero Design**
Designer: **Steve Trapero**

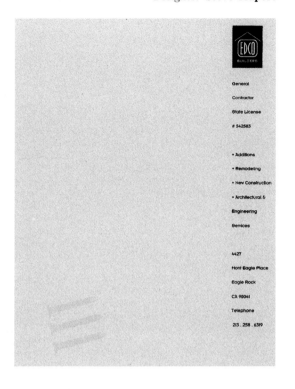

GeoCapital

GeoCapital Corporation   767 Fifth Avenue, New York, NY 10153-4900   tel (212) 486-6495 • fax (212) 486-4409

Client: **GeoCapital Corporation**
Design Firm: **Mike Quon Design Office**
Designers: **Mike Quon, Erick Kuo**

Client: **IDIOM**
Design Firm: **Aerial**
Designers: **Tracy Moon, Michelle Gottlieb**

id´i·om

1. 431 Jackson Street 2. San Francisco, California 94111-1601 3. Telephone 415.788.7210 4. Facsimile 415.982.2276

Client: **Oklahoma Human Resources Conference**
Design Firm: **Michael J. O'Keefe**
Designers: **Michael J. O'Keefe, Tim Watson**

Client: **Art O Mat Design**
Design Firm: **Art O Mat Design**
Designers: **Jacki McCarthy, Mark Kaufman**

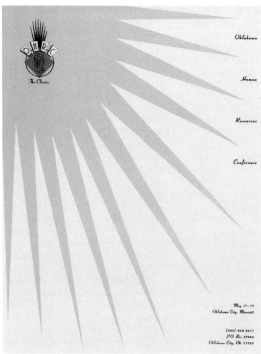

Client: **Dick Patrick Studios**
Design Firm: **Swieter Design United States**
Designer: **Mark Ford**

Corporate
Identity Manuals

Client: **Sunkist Growers, Inc.**
Design Firm: **Landor Associates**
Designers: **Bill Chiaravalle, Sabrina Saure**

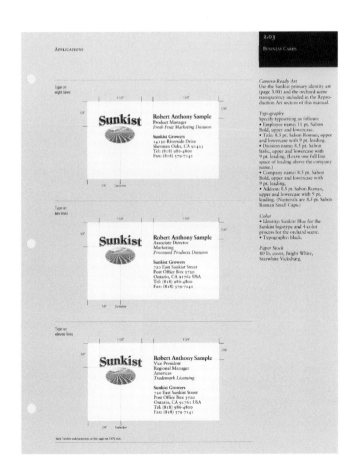

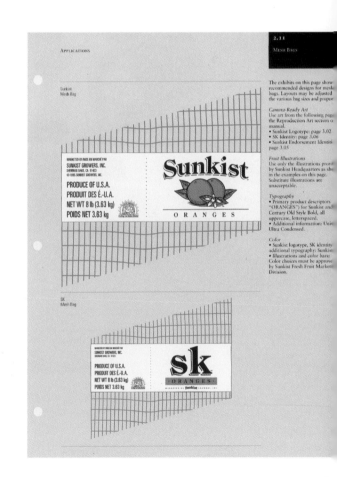

Client: **Converse**
Design Firm: **Jager Di Paola Kemp Design**
Designers: **Michael Jager, Janet Johnson,**
Christopher Vice, Keith Brown

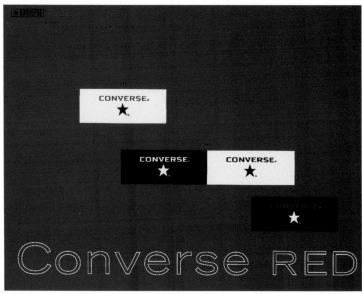

Client: **Flagstar (Denny's)**
Design Firm: **King Casey, Inc.**
Designers: **John Chrzanowski, Steve Brent**

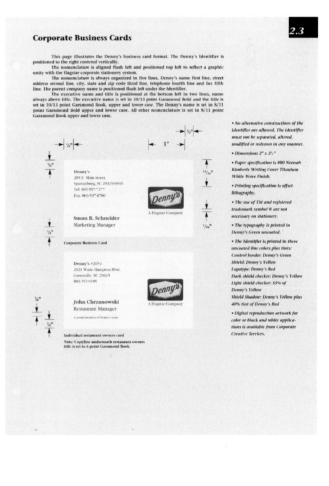

Corporate Business Cards

This page illustrates the Denny's business card format. The Denny's Identifier is positioned to the right centered vertically.

The nomenclature is aligned flush left and positioned top left to reflect a graphic unity with the Flagstar corporate stationery system.

The nomenclature is always organized in five lines, Denny's name first line, street address second line, city, state and zip code third line, telephone fourth line and fax fifth line. The parent company name is positioned flush left under the Identifier.

The executive name and title is positioned at the bottom left in two lines, name always above title. The executive name is set in 10/13 point Garamond Bold and the title is set in 10/13 point Garamond Book, upper and lower case. The Denny's name is set in 8/11 point Garamond Bold upper and lower case. All other nomenclature is set in 8/11 point Garamond Book upper and lower case.

Denny's
205 E. Main Street
Spartanburg, SC 29319-9945
Tel: 803-597-7277
Fax: 803-597-8790

Susan R. Schneider
Marketing Manager

A Flagstar Company

Corporate Business Card

Denny's #2054
2924 Wade Hampton Blvd.
Greenville, SC 29615
803-392-9105

John Chrzanowski
Restaurant Manager

A proud member of Denny's team

A Flagstar Company

Individual restaurant owners card
Note: Copyline underneath restaurant owners
title is set in 6 point Garamond Book.

• *No alternative constructions of the Identifier are allowed. The Identifier must not be separated, altered, modified or redrawn in any manner.*

• *Dimensions 2" x 3½"*

• *Paper specification is #80 Neenah Kimberly Writing Cover Titanium White Wove Finish.*

• *Printing specification is offset lithography.*

• *The use of TM and registered trademark symbol ® are not necessary on stationery.*

• *The typography is printed in Denny's Green uncoated.*

• *The Identifier is printed in three uncoated line colors plus this:*
Control border: Denny's Green
Shield: Denny's Yellow
Logotype: Denny's Red
Dark shield checker: Denny's Yellow
Light shield checker: 55% of Denny's Yellow
Shield Shadow: Denny's Yellow plus 40% tint of Denny's Red

• *Digital reproduction artwork for color or black and white applications is available from Corporate Creative Services.*

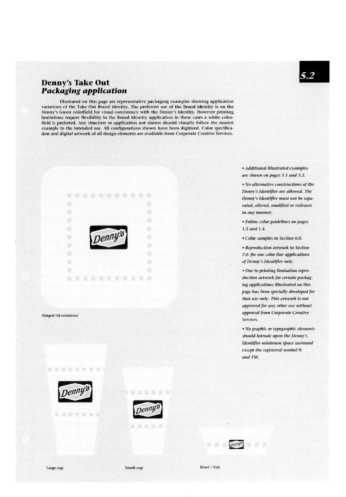

Denny's Take Out
Packaging application

Illustrated on this page are representative packaging examples showing application variations of the Take Out Brand identity. The preferred use of the Brand identity is on the Denny's Green colorfield for visual consistency with the Denny's identity. However printing limitations require flexibility in the Brand identity application in these cases a white colorfield is preferred. Any structure or application not shown should visually follow the nearest example to the intended use. All configurations shown have been digitized. Color specification and digital artwork of all design elements are available from Corporate Creative Services.

Hinged lid container

• *Additional illustrated examples are shown on pages 5.1 and 5.3.*

• *No alternative constructions of the Denny's Identifier are allowed. The Denny's Identifier must not be separated, altered, modified or redrawn in any manner.*

• *Follow color guidelines on pages 1.3 and 1.4.*

• *Color samples in Section 6.0.*

• *Reproduction artwork in Section 7.0 for one color line applications of Denny's Identifier only.*

• *Due to printing limitation reproduction artwork for certain packaging applications illustrated on this page has been specially developed for that use only. This artwork is not approved for any other use without approval from Corporate Creative Services.*

• *No graphic or typographic elements should intrude upon the Denny's Identifier minimum space surround except the registered symbol ® and TM.*

Large cup   Small cup   Bowl / Tub

187

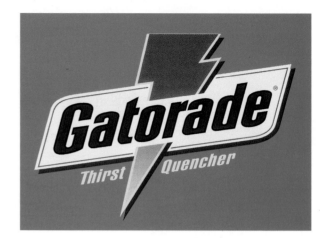

Client: **Gatorade**
Design Firm: **Landor Associates**
Designers: **Jon Weden, Henrik Olsen**

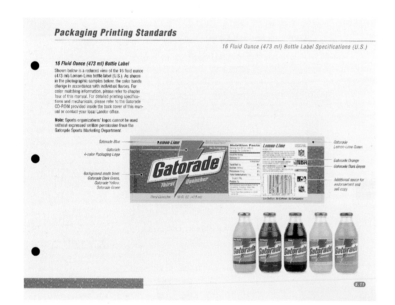

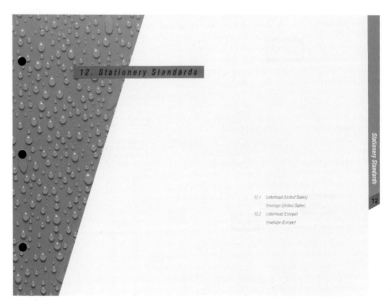

188

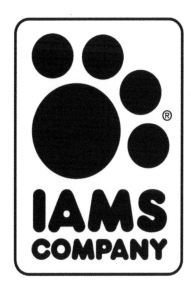

Client: **The Iams Company**
Design Firm: **Seta Appleman & Showell**
Designer: **Jeff Fulwiler**

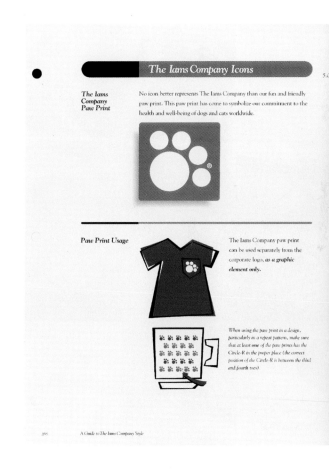

The Iams Company Paw Print

No icon better represents The Iams Company than our fun and friendly paw print. This paw print has come to symbolize our commitment to the health and well-being of dogs and cats worldwide.

Paw Print Usage

The Iams Company paw print can be used separately from the corporate logo, *as a graphic element only.*

When using the paw print in a design, particularly in a repeat pattern, make sure that at least one of the paw prints has the Circle-R in the proper place (the correct position of the Circle-R is between the third and fourth toes).

A Guide to The Iams Company Style

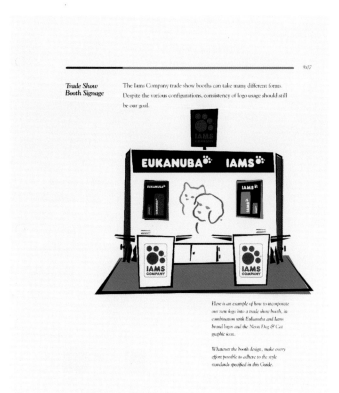

Trade Show Booth Signage

The Iams Company trade show booths can take many different forms. Despite the various configurations, consistency of logo usage should still be our goal.

Here is an example of how to incorporate our new logo into a trade show booth, in combination with Eukanuba and Iams brand logos and the Neon Dog & Cat graphic icon.

Whatever the booth design, make every effort possible to adhere to the style standards specified in this Guide.

A Guide to The Iams Company Style

189

Client: **National Semiconductor**
Design Firm: **Casper Design Group**
Designers: **Charlene Tiani, Anderson Gin**

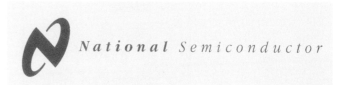

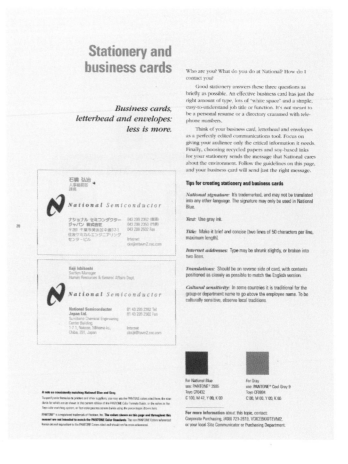

New York
Mercantile Exchange

NYMEX/COMEX. Two divisions, one marketplace

Client: **New York Mercantile Exchange**
Design Firm: **Cullinane Design, Inc.**
Designers: **Bob Cullinane, Yasemin Cullinane**

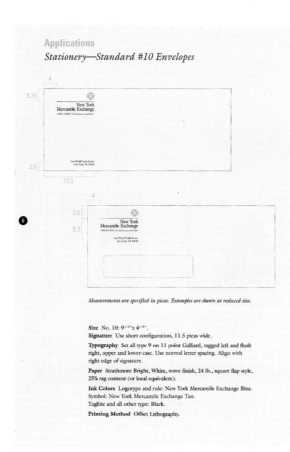

Applications
Stationery—Standard #10 Envelopes

Measurements are specified in picas. Examples are shown at reduced size.

Size No. 10: 9¹/²˝x 4¹/8˝.

Signature Use short configuration, 11.5 picas wide.

Typography Set all type 9 on 11 point Galliard, ragged left and flush right, upper and lower-case. Use normal letter spacing. Align with right edge of signature.

Paper Strathmore Bright, White, wove finish, 24 lb., square flap style, 25% rag content (or local equivalent).

Ink Colors Logotype and rule: New York Mercantile Exchange Blue. Symbol: New York Mercantile Exchange Tan. Tagline and all other type: Black.

Printing Method Offset Lithography.

Basic Identity Standards
Placement and Incorrect Use

Whenever incorporating the signature into any communication align it with a dominant axis in the design, such as the placement of type, photos, or color fields.

Shown below are examples of communications materials that demonstrate correct placement of the signature.

Careless treatment of the signature obscures the firm's identity

and reduces the effectiveness of the communication.

The uses shown below reduce its impact and therefore should be avoided.

Do not change alignment of the signature components.

Do not enclose the signature in a surrounding shape.

Do not reposition the signature components.

Do not run the logotype on one line.

Careless treatment of the signature obscures the firm's identity and reduces the effectiveness of the communication.

191

STJOHN
Health System

Client: **St. John Health System**
Design Firm: **Ford & Earl Associates, Inc.**
Designers: **Bonnie Detloff-Zielinski,**
  Susan J. Garrett

Client: **Stream International**
Design Firm: **Clifford Selbert Design Collaborative**
Designers: **Lynn Riddle, Bill Crosby, April Skinnard**

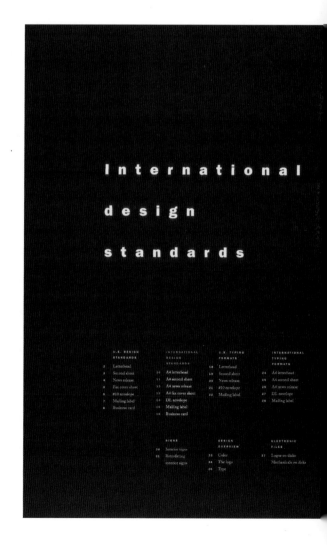

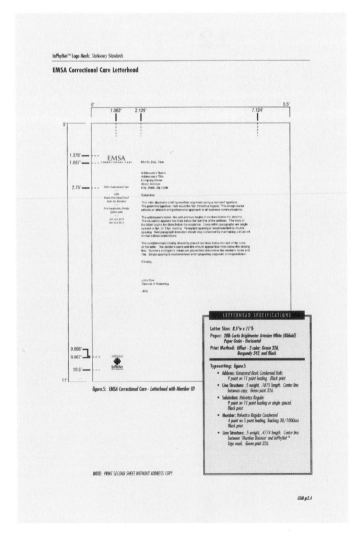

Client: **InPhyNet Medical Management**
Design Firm: **The Dunn Design Group**
Designers: **Richard D. Juenger, Richard W. Juenger**

STATIONERY STANDARDS

Client: **Northwest Community Healthcare**
Design Firm: **Moira & Company**
Designer: **Ilse Krause**

Smaller brochures or folders may be most appropriate for specific communication needs, such as product and program promotions.

When space allows – the inclusion of a map on the back panel helps to identify NCH's many service locations.

Contact the Marketing Communications department for assistance prior to producing any publication.

Publications
3.625 in. x 8.5 in.

4.5

Northwest Community Healthcare advertising should be flexible, based on the communication objectives for the ad, and therefore includes a wide range of sizes. NCH advertising should be designed with a unifying look. Representative sample layouts are shown later in this section as a reference for overall consistency.

As in all communications materials, to help create a consistent and recognizable identity for the advertising generated by NCH, the Futura family and the Garamond family of type should be used consistently as the primary supporting typefaces on all advertising.

Headlines should be brief and concise in order to maximize type size.

Photography or illustration may be used if appropriate and the budget permits.

Contact the Marketing Communications department for assistance prior to producing any advertisement.

Advertising

6.1   Ad Signature
6.2   Product Advertising
6.3   Recruitment Advertising
6.4   Corporate Advertising

6

Client: **Summit Properties**
Design Firm: **Lester and Associates**
Designers: **David Lester, Chris Bowles**

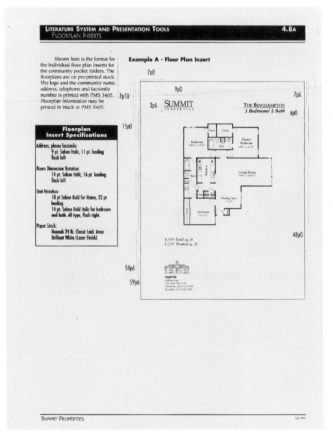

**Jameson
Care Center**

A Member of Jameson Health System

Client: **Jameson Health System**
Design Firm: **Adam Filippo & Associates**
Designer: **Barbara Peak Long**

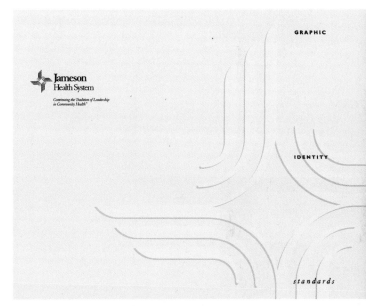

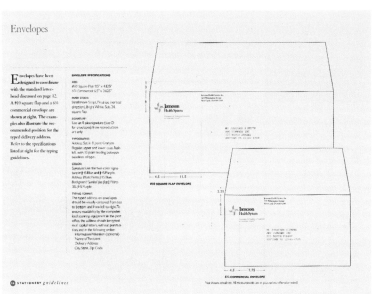

Client: **Burton Snowboards**
Design Firm: **Jager Di Paola Kemp Design**
Designers: **Michael Jager, David Covell,**
  John Phemister

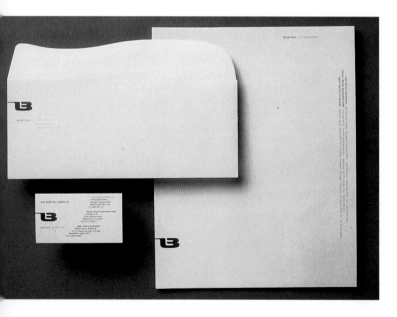

Client: **Chemical Banking Corporation**
Design Firm: **R.A. Danzig, Inc.**
Designer: **Jessica Danzig**

Overview

As of the print date below, Chemical's current campaign specifies use of the following typefaces.

Headlines

The preferred typeface for headlines is Trajan bold, which only sets in all caps. Typeface should be specified as large/ small caps with the small caps equal to 75% of the large caps.

The typeface should always be specified as initial caps and condensed 76%.

Body Copy

Janson text is the recommended typeface for body copy with a minimum of one point leading. Typeface should be specified as upper/lower case and condensed 76%.

Legal Footnotes

All legal footnotes must be set in Helvetica regular, 7 point solid, upper/ lower case, flush left and rag right.

Approval Source

If an alternate typeface seems appropriate, contact either:

Claudia Mengel, VP
Creative Services
600 Fifth Avenue, 6th floor
New York, NY 10020
Telephone # – (212) 332-3870
Fax # – (212) 332-3865; or

Seth Lederman, VP
Creative Services
600 Fifth Avenue, 6th Floor
New York, NY 10020
Telephone # – (212) 332-3872
Fax # – (212) 332-3865

THIS IS AN EXAMPLE OF TRAJAN BOLD WITH LARGE AND SMALL CAPS CONDENSED 76%.

Preferred typeface for headlines

This is an example of Janson text condensed 76%. This is an example of Janson text condensed 76%.

Preferred typeface for body copy

This is an example of Helvetica regular. This is an example of Helvetica regular.

Typeface for legal footnotes

On certain computer systems, 75% represents the automatic default.

May, 1995   U.S. Domestic – 6.1

Customer Materials
Identification Format

Legal Signatures

...continued

Relationship
In legal signatures, the precise placement of both the subsidiary's legal name and the rule must be in fixed proportion and specific relationship to the Corporate Signature.

Production Method
To create a legal signature:

Determine the size required for corporate identification by following the guidelines specified in the appropriate sections of this chapter;

Select the closest larger size Corporate Signature from an authorized reproduction sheet or disk;² then

Position the appropriate weight rule, according to Exhibit H in this section; and

Position the appropriately sized legal name according to guidelines specified further on in this section.

When produced in this manner, the legal signature can be reduced as a unit to the required size, thereby ensuring that the proportions remain constant and the required relationships are maintained.

Positioning the Rule
In both acceptable formats of a signature, the precise position of the rule is determined by:

Aligning the left edge of the rule flush left with the initial "C" in Chemical; and

Aligning the base of the rule with the base of the Graphic Symbol.

In the format shown in Exhibit C, the right edge of the rule extends to the point that is exactly one-half the width of the last column on the right of the grid for the specific customer material being developed.

In the format shown in Exhibit D, the right edge of the rule is flush right with either the Chemical Logotype or the subsidiary's legal name, whichever is longer.

In both formats, the weight of the rule is in direct proportion to the pica width of the Chemical Logotype. Proportionate weights are indicated in Exhibit H further on in this section.

Exhibit C

Preferred legal signature format

The minimum clearance area after the "L" in Chemical must be equal to the height of the small caps in the Chemical Logotype.

Exhibit D

CHEMICAL
Subsidiary's Legal Name

If preferred, individual legal signatures can be obtained from Creative Services. Contact either Claudia Mengel or Seth Lederman, as referenced in the Introduction to this chapter.
²The pica widths of the Chemical Logotypes on each reproduction sheet and disk correspond to those included in Exhibit H further on in this section.

continued...

May, 1995   U.S. Domestic – 4.4

Client: **Reltec Corporation**
Design Firm: **Media II**
Designers: **Roy Harry, Janet Dodrill**

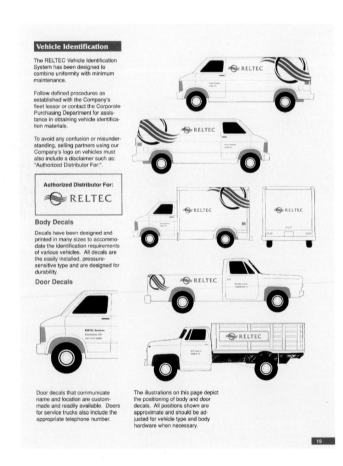

Vehicle Identification

The RELTEC Vehicle Identification System has been designed to combine uniformity with minimum maintenance.

Follow defined procedures as established with the Company's fleet lessor or contact the Corporate Purchasing Department for assistance in obtaining vehicle identification materials.

To avoid any confusion or misunderstanding, selling partners using our Company's logo on vehicles must also include a disclaimer such as: "Authorized Distributor For:".

Authorized Distributor For:

⬲ RELTEC

Body Decals

Decals have been designed and printed in many sizes to accommodate the identification requirements of various vehicles. All decals are the easily installed, pressure-sensitive type and are designed for durability.

Door Decals

Door decals that communicate name and location are custom-made and readily available. Doors for service trucks also include the appropriate telephone number.

The illustrations on this page depict the positioning of body and door decals. All positions shown are approximate and should be adjusted for vehicle type and body hardware when necessary.

19

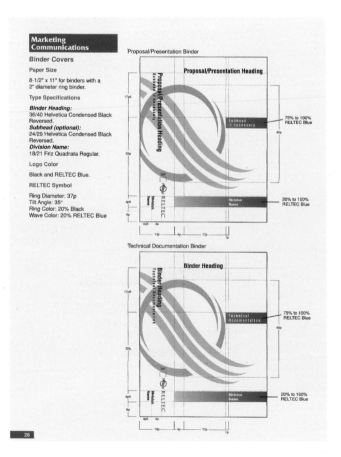

Marketing Communications

Binder Covers

Paper Size

8-1/2" x 11" for binders with a 2" diameter ring binder.

Type Specifications

Binder Heading:
36/40 Helvetica Condensed Black Reversed.
Subhead (optional):
24/29 Helvetica Condensed Black Reversed.
Division Name:
18/21 Friz Quadrata Regular.

Logo Color

Black and RELTEC Blue.

RELTEC Symbol

Ring Diameter: 37p
Tilt Angle: 35°
Ring Color: 20% Black
Wave Color: 20% RELTEC Blue

28

200

CELEBRATION
DAYTON '96™

Client: **City of Dayton, CD '96**
Design Firm: **Visual Marketing Associates**
Designer: **Lynn Sampson**

STAMPS / CALENDARS / POSTERS

Commemorative stamps, calendars and posters are just a small sampling of the multitude of print work applications that will be designed and produced for the bicentennial celebration.

The layout and color breaks on print work applications should emphasize the underlying square grid. Whenever possible, high contrast photography should be incorporated and display type should always be set in Univers 49.

There will be three poster formats — all of which are equal to 1 x 1.5 square proportions.

The largest format (25" x 37.5") will be used for official bicentennial commemorative posters and major event posters.

The medium size (20" x 30") will be used for special registered events scheduled throughout the celebration.

The smallest format (15" x 22.5") will be used primarily for smaller neighborhood events.

BANNERS

Festive banners will be used for maximum impact throughout downtown Dayton and surrounding areas. Some banners will be event specific, while others may be more general or timeless. To increase the life of such banners, detachable panels will be incorporated for the "Celebration Dayton" logo. The logo panel can then be removed completely from the banner structure after the bicentennial celebration or a new logo or sign can be used in place of the CD '96 logo so that the banners may still be used beyond 1996.

When laying out the design of the banners, the double square proportion should be emphasized by using color breaks, pattern and/or border details. Text should be minimal but imagery and color should have high impact.

Signage and Environmental Graphics

Client: **The Library, Ltd.—bookstore**
Design Firm: **CUBE Advertising/Design**
Designer: **David Chiow**

Client: **Coffee Coffee**
Design Firm: **Advertising Design, Inc.**
Designer: **Dennis Boyd**

Client: **Signworks**
Design Firm: **Design Services, Inc.**
Designers: **Rod Parker, Lonnie Carnaggio**

Client: **Self (store fixturing show)**
Design Firm: **Design Forum**
Designers: **Bill Chidley, Dave Nixon, Scott Jeffrey**

Client: **Iomega Corporation**
Design Firm: **Fitch, Inc.**
Designers: **Jaimie Alexander, Paul Lycett,
Eric Weissinger, Paul Lechleiter**

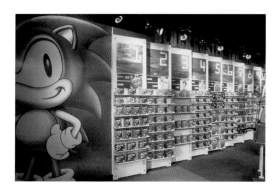

Client: **Blockbuster Entertainment Corporation**
Design Firm: **Fitch, Inc.**
Designers: **Paul Lechleiter, Mark Artus, Fred Goode, Jeff Pacione**

Client: **Westland Town Center**
Design Firm: **Copeland Hirthler design + communications**
Designers: **Brad Copeland, George Hirthler**

Client: **Disney Development Corporation
Disney's All Star Resorts**
Design Firm: **Communication Arts, Inc.**
Designers: **Patricia Van Hook, Richard Fox, Gary Kushner**

Client: **University of Colorado**
Design Firm: **Communication Arts, Inc.**
Designers: **Richard Fox, Max Steele,
Karl Hirschmann, Margaret Sewell**

Client: **J. Gilberts**
Design Firm: **MULLER + Company**
Designers: **Jon Simonsen,
David Shultz**

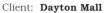

Client: **Dayton Mall**
Design Firm: **FRCH Design Worldwide**
Designers: **Michael Beeghly, Charles Aenlle, Erik Brown**

Client: **Clark Oil**
Design Firm: **Antista Fairclough Design**
Designers: **Tom Antista, Thomas Fairclough**

Client: **The City of National City, California**
Design Firm: **Nicholson Design**
Designer: **Joe C. Nicholson**

Client: **Straits Steamship Land Ptl.**
Design Firm: **Communication Arts, Inc.**
Designers: **Richard Foy, John Ward, Phil Reed, Lydia Young, T. Keith Harley**

Client: **B. Dalton Bookseller**
Design Firm: **Kiku Obata + Company**
Designers: **Idie McGinty, Tim McGinty, Pam Bliss, Jane McKneely**

Client: **Chesapeake Bagel Bakery**
Design Firm: **Kiku Obata & Company**
Designers: **Kiku Obata, Tim McGinty, Jane McNeely, Theresa Henrekin, James Keane**

Client: **Faison Associates**
Design Firm: **T L Horton Design, Inc.**
Designer: **Tony L. Horton**

Client: **Ripplesteins**
Design Firm: **Vaughn Wedeen Creative, Inc.**
Designer: **Rick Vaughn**

Client: **Escondido—California Center for the Arts**
Design Firm: **Nicholson Design**
Designer: **Joe C. Nicholson**

Client: **Genesee Brewing Company**
Design Firm: **McElveney & Palozzi Graphic Design Group**
Designer: **Matthew Nowicki**

Client: **Metropolitan District**
Design Firm: **HNTB Corporation**
Designers: **Robert Hurst, Jane True, Chris Lanza**

Client: **S.R. Hoeft Direct**
Design Firm: **Metropolis Design**
Designer: **Andy Quevreaux**

Client: **Dreyer's Grand Ice Cream**
Design Firm: **Monnens-Addis Design**
Designers: **Debbie Smith, Terry Dudley,
Joel Glenn, Leila Daubert**

Client: **WEFX 95.9 FM "The Fox"**
Design Firm: **Cullinane Design, Inc.**
Designers: **Robert Cullinane,
Michael McCaffery**

Client: **A&P Food Stores**
Design Firm: **Words and Pictures**
Designers: **Smita Aggarwal, Angela Vairo,
Rhonda Smith**

Client: **Kenneth Cole Productions**
Design Firm: **FRCH Design Worldwide**
Designer: **Susan Menk**

Client: **Blockbuster Entertainment Corporation**
Design Firm: **Fitch, Inc.**
Designers: **Paul Lechleiter, Mark Artus,
Beth Dorsey, Kian Huat Kuan**

Client: **Key Bank**
Design Firm: **FRCH Design Worldwide**
Designers: **Steven McGowan, Joan Donnelly,
Tessa Westermeyer, Dan Enwright**

Client: **The McGraw-Hill Companies**
Design Firm: **Lippincott & Margulies**
Designers: **Connie Birdsall, Jane Ashley**

Client: **New Boston Garden Corporation**
Design Firm: **Fitch, Inc.**
Designers: **Bob Wolsfelt, Randall Sckaal**

Client: **San Jose Mercury News**
Design Firm: **Patt Mann Berry Design**
Designers: **Patt Mann Berry,
Chris Cross, Charlene Li**

Client: **Northwest Plaza**
Design Firm: **FRCH Design Worldwide**
Designers: **Michael Beeghly, Martin Treu, Raymond Berberich**

Client: **Royal Crown Cola Co.**
Design Firm: **Antista Fairclough Design**
Designers: **Tom Antista, Thomas Fairclough**

Client: **Winmar Company, Inc.**
Washington Square Mall
Design Firm: **Design Partnerhsip/Portland**
Designer: **K. Ambrosini**

Client: **Progressive Bagel Concepts**
Design Firm: **Fitch, Inc.**
Designers: **Mark Artus, Christian Davies,**
Paul Lechleiter

Client: **Taco John**
Design Firm: **Addison Seefeld and Brew**
Designer: **Cindy Goefft**

Client: **Westfield, Inc.**
Design Firm: **T L Horton Design, Inc.**
Designer: **Tony L. Horton**

Client: **Disney Development Corp.**
Design Firm: **Communication Arts, Inc.**
Designers: **Dave Tweed, Richard Foy,**
Gary Kushner

Client: **Bancomer**
Design Firm: **Addison Seefeld and Brew**
Designers: **Paul Daddino, Patrick Poinsot**

Client: **American Express Travel Related Services**
Design Firm: **Cullinane Design, Inc.**
Designer: **Yasemin Cullinane**

Client: **Mick's**
Design Firm: **Copeland Hirthler design + communications**
Designers: **Brad Copeland, George Hirthler,**
Suzy Miller, Sarah Huie

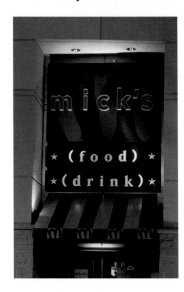

Client: **Rollerblade**
Design Firm: **Minneapolis Design Company**
Designer: **Robert Warren Carlson**

Corporate
Image Brochures

Client: **The Sloan Group**
Design Firm: **The Sloan Group**
Designer: **Wyndy Wilder**

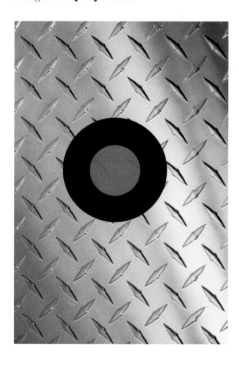

Client: **California Museum of Science and Industry**
Design Firm: **Douglas Oliver Design Office**
Designer: **Douglas Oliver, Robin Weaver**

Client: **Graef + Ziller Design**
Design Firm: **Graef + Ziller Design**
Designers: **Andrew Graef, Barbara Ziller**

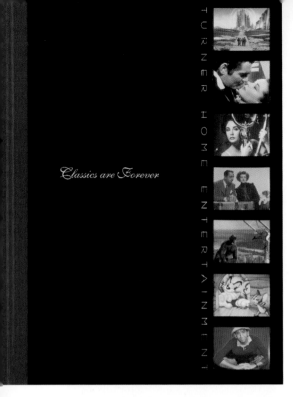

Client: **Turner Entertainment**
Classics are Forever
Design Firm: **The Sloan Group**
Designer: **Wyndy Wilder**

Client: **Columbia Crest Winery**
Design Firm: **Hornall Anderson Design Works, Inc.**
Designers: **John Hornall, Debra Hampton,**
Mary Chin Hutchison, Viola Lehr

Client: **Towers Perrin**
Design Firm: **Sean Michael Edwards**
Designer: **Ken Barber**

Client: **Lino Graphic Services**
Design Firm: **Graphic Concepts Group**
Designer: **Brian Wilburn**

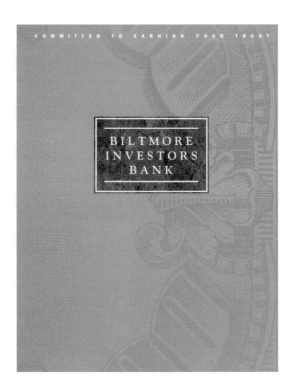

HIRAI SEIMITSU CORPORATION

Client: **Hirai Seimitsu Corporation**
Design Firm: **Hiroshi Hamada Design Studio**
Designer: **Hiroshi Hamada**

Client: **Johnson International, Inc.**
Design Firm: **Jack Weiss Associates**
Designer: **Jack Weiss**

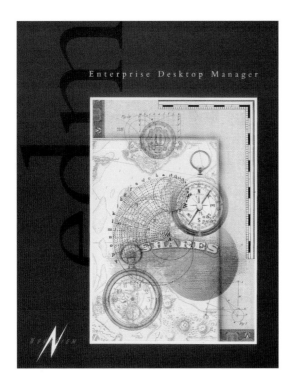

Client: **Novadigm, Inc.**
Design Firm: **Kawalek & Associates**
Designer: **Margaret Swart**

Client: **UFP Technologies**
Design Firm: **Imageset**
Designer: **Mary Reed**

Client: **News America FSI Division**
Design Firm: **Ziccardi & Partners, Inc.**
Designer: **Vicki Wolliver**

Client: **SVO Specialty Products, Inc.**
Design Firm: **Olson and Gibbons, Inc.**
Designer: **Tom Ladyga**

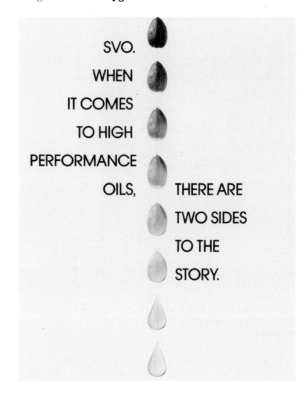

SVO. WHEN IT COMES TO HIGH PERFORMANCE OILS, THERE ARE TWO SIDES TO THE STORY.

Client: **Ketchum Public Relations**
Ormet Capabilities Brochure
Design Firm: **John Brady Design Consultants**
Designers: **Mona MacDonald, Sharon Bretz**

Client: **Balmar Legal**
Design Firm: **Greenfield/Belser**
Designer: **Chris Leonard**

Crisis Management

214

Client: **Apple Computer Co.**
Design Firm: **WaterWork Art**
Designer: **Jim Rudolph**

Addison

Client: **Addison Seefeld and Brew**
Design Firm: **Addison Seefeld and Brew**
Designer: **Micaela Merce**

Client: **Western Atlas, Inc.**
Design Firm: **The Jefferies Association**
Designers: **Ron Jefferies and John Tom**

Client: **Disclosure, Inc.**
Design Firm: **Lomangino Studio, Inc.**
Designer: **Alain Delille Blunt**

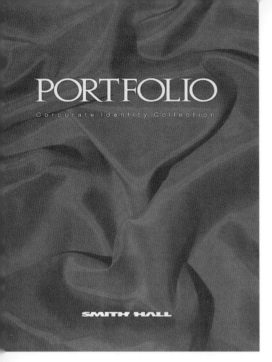

PORTFOLIO
Corporate Identity Collection

SMITH HALL

Client: **Smith & Hall**
Design Firm: **Smith & Hall**
Designer: **Dann Hall**

Client: **Computer Science Corporation**
Design Firm: **CSC Graphic Design**
Designer: **Roy Juan**

EXPANDING BUSINESS HORIZONS

with Multimedia

CSC

Client: **Equifax**
Design Firm: **Copeland Hirthler design + communications**
Designers: **Brad Copeland, Melanie Bass, David Woodward, Shawn Briasfield**

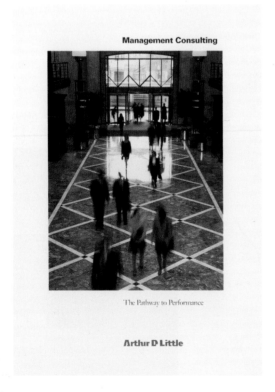

Management Consulting

The Pathway to Performance

Arthur D Little

Client: **Arthur D. Little, Inc.**
Design Firm: **Arthur D. Little Corporate Marketing**
Designer: **Karen Stockert**

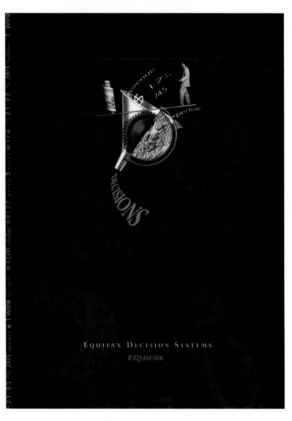

DECISIONS

EQUIFAX DECISION SYSTEMS
EQUIFAX

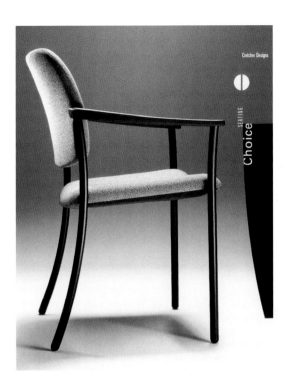

Client: **Cretcher Designs**
Design Firm: **Michael Orr + Associates, Inc.**
Designers: **Michael R. Orr, Gregory Duell**

Client: **W. Kurt Feick/Dynamic Hedge, Inc.**
Design Firm: **Halcyon Endeavours**
Designer: **Shelley Heller**

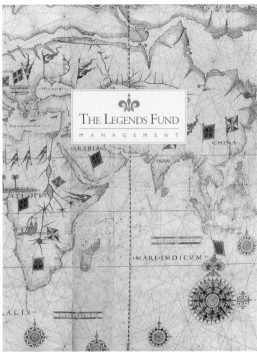

Client: **Cretcher Designs**
Design Firm: **Michael Orr + Associates, Inc.**
Designers: **Michael R. Orr, Gregory Duell**

Client: **Bigsby & Kruthers**
Design Firm: **Deborah Schneider Design**
Designer: **Deborah Schneider**

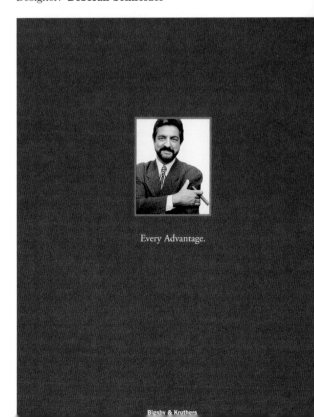

Client: **Boston Institutional Services, Inc.**
Design Firm: **Belviso Creative Services**
Designers: **Bob Belviso, Larry Yannes**

Client: **Follett Software Company Automation Guide**
Design Firm: **Esdale Associates, Inc.**
Designers: **Margaret Carsello, Susan Esdale**

Client: **World Color Press**
Design Firm: **Copeland Hirthler design + communications**
Designers: **Brad Copeland, Todd Brooks, Kathy Roberts**

Client: **ATL**
Design Firm: **Floathe Johnson**
Designers: **Dan Bockman, John Engerman**

218

Client: **Adaptec**
Design Firm: **Lee/McCoy & Assoc.**
Designers: **Cindy Lee, Deanne Furuta**

Client: **Pecos—Playing to Win**
Design Firm: **Vaughn Wedeen Creative, Inc.**
Designer: **Rick Vaughn**

Client: **Pape-Dawson Engineers**
Design Firm: **Eickhoff Hannan Rue**
Designer: **Mark A. Rue**

Client: **DPR Construction, Inc.**
Design Firm: **Casper Design Group**
Designers: **Anderson Gin, Charlene Tiani**

Client: **FX Networks**
Design Firm: **BRD Design**
Designer: **Peter King Robbins**

Client: **Ambrosi & Associates, Inc.**
Design Firm: **Ambrosi & Associates, Inc.**

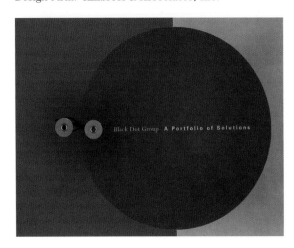

Client: **MAPP Construction, Inc.**
Design Firm: **Design Services, Inc.**
Designers: **Rod Parker, Lonnie Carnaggio**

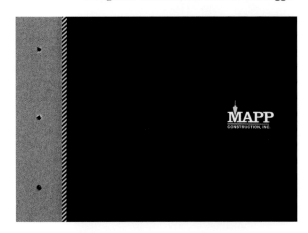

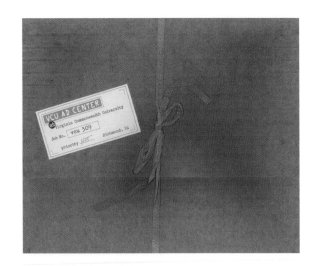

Client: **VCU Ad Center**
Design Firm: **O'Keefe Marketing**
Designer: **Jeff Schaich**

Client: **Macromedia**
Design Firm: **Elliott/Dickens**
Designers: **Craig Elliott, Ken Dickens, Helen Finkenstaedt**

Client: **Metaphase Design Group**
Design Firm: **Pheonix Creative, St. Louis**
Designer: **Ed Mantels-Seeker**

220

We are committed to helping your
people work more effectively. How?
By integrating the goals of your
organization, the technology you use
and how your people work in the
space they occupy. This focus governs
all our research efforts and the
products, services and expertise we
provide through our independent,
worldwide dealer network.

Steelcase

Client: **Steelcase, Inc.**
Design Firm: **Corbin Design**
Designers: **Mark Vanderklipp, Jeffry Corbin**

Client: **Spaulding & Slye**
Design Firm: **Greenfield/Belser**
Designer: **Chris Leonard**

Client: **VHA, Inc.**
Design Firm: **Tocquigny Advertising and Design**
Designers: **Lori Walls, David Martino**

Client: **ad:tech**
   an advertising technology trade show
Design Firm: **O'Keefe Marketing**
Designer: **Jeff Schaich**

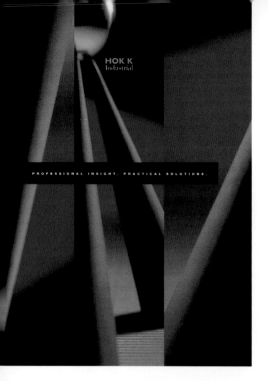

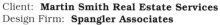

Client: **Martin Smith Real Estate Services**
Design Firm: **Spangler Associates**
Designer: **Susan Mendenhall**

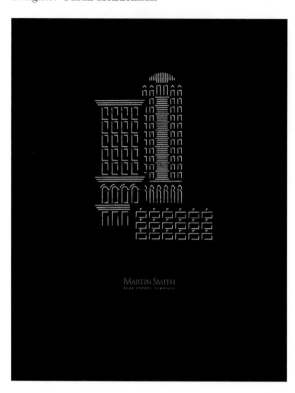

Client: **HOK/K Industrial**
Design Firm: **Kearns Design, Inc.**
Designer: **Bart Caylor**

Client: **Chase Manhattan Bank**
Design Firm: **Mike Quon Design Office**
Designer: **Mike Quon**

Client: **PacLease**
Design Firm: **Phinney/Bischoff Design House**
Designer: **Dean Hart**

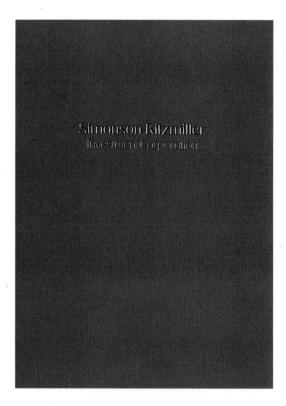

Client: **Simonson-Kitzmiller Investment Corporation**
Design Firm: **The Rogers Group, Inc.**
Designer: **Don Rogers**

Client: **Otis Spunkmeyer, Inc.**
Design Firm: **Profile Design**
Designers: **Tom McNulty, Brian Jacobson**

Client: **Whittman-Hart, L.P.**
Design Firm: **Roman Design**
Designer: **Lisa Romanowski**

Client: **Telecel**
Design Firm: **King Casey, Inc.**
Designers: **John Chrzanowski,
Steve Brent**

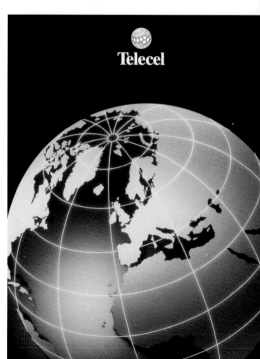

Client: **Harman Kardon International**
Design Firm: **Fitch, Inc.**
Designers: **Ann Gildea, Kate Murphy, Brooks Beisch, Michael Mooney**

Client: **Corbis—merchandising brochures**
Design Firm: **Hornall Anderson Design Works, Inc.**
Designers: **Jack Anderson, John Anicker, David Bates, Mary Hermes**

Client: **Pottery Barn**
Design Firm: **Arias Associates**
Designers: **Mauricio Arias, Karin Bryant**

Client: **Lowell School**
Design Firm: **Greenfield/Belser**
Designer: **Burkey Belser**

Client: **US West Record Performance**
Design Firm: **Vaughn Wedeen Creative, Inc.**
Designers: **Steve Wedeen, Lucy Hitchcock**

Client: **Luxtron**
Design Firm: **Lee/McCoy & Assoc.**
Designers: **Laura Bauer, Cindy Lee**

Client: **Ichiban Records**
Design Firm: **Ichiban Records Art Department**
Designers: **Francis P. Dreyer III, Cole Gerst**

Client: **Primo Angeli, Inc.**
Design Firm: **Primo Angeli, Inc.**
Designers: **Vicki Olds, Terrence Tong,
Primo Angeli**

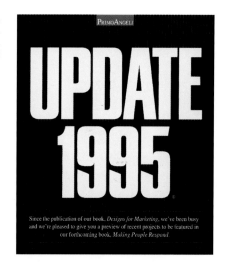

Client: **Lithographics, Inc.**
Design Firm: **Keiler Design Group**
Designer: **Jeff Lin**

Client: **FHP Health Care/Life Cycles brochure**
Design Firm: **Sanft Design, Inc.**
Designers: **Alfred Sanft, Paul Howell, David Rengifo**

Design Firm: **"In-House"
Seasonal Specialties Company**
Designers: **Jennifer, Sheeler, Barbara Roth**

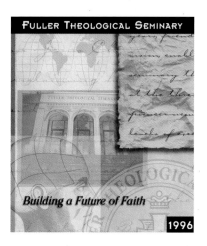

Client: **Fuller Theological Seminary**
Design Firm: **Artime, Crane & Company**
Designers: **Henry Artime, Denver Minnich**

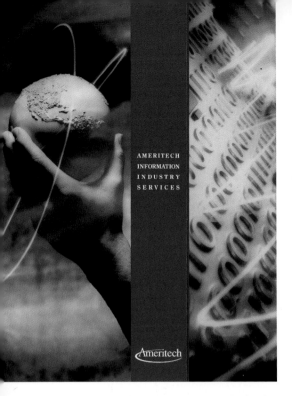

Client: **Ameritech Information
Industry Services**
Design Firm: **Esdale Associates, Inc.**
Designers: **Margaret Carsello, Susan K. Esdale**

Client: **Expersoft Corporation**
Design Firm: **Abrams Design Group**
Designer: **Kim Ferrell**

Client: **The National Science Foundation**
Design Firm: **Brandegee, Inc.**
Designers: **Brian Lee Campbell, Richard A. Hooper**

Client: **CBT Systems, Inc.**
Design Firm: **Three Marketeers Advertising, Inc.**
Designers: **Greg Campbell, Amelia Rodrigues, Tracy Power,
Dena DelAngelo**

226

Client: **Norwest Bank**
Design Firm: **Design One**
Designers: **Jim Fash, Jacqueline Ghosin, Franz Platte, Alisa Rudloff, Chris Peterson**

Client: **Hitachi Data Systems**
Design Firm: **HDS Creative Services**
Designer: **Mikyong Han**

Client: **Hitachi Data Systems**
Design Firm: **HDS Creative Services**
Designer: **Mikyong Han**

Client: **E! Entertainment Television**
Design Firm: **BRD Design**
Designers: **Peter King Robbins, Dan Evans**

Client: **University of Southern California**
Design Firm: **Clifford Selbert**
Design Collaborative
Designers: **Brian Lane, Jeff Breidenbach**

Client: **Frank Russell Company**
Design Firm: **Hornall Anderson Design Works, Inc.**
Designers: **Jack Anderson, Lisa Cerveny, Suzanne Haddon**

Client: **Morgan Lewis & Bockius**
Design Firm: **Greenfield/Belser**
Designer: **Amy Darragh**

Client: **Microsoft**
Design Firm: **Giordano Kearfott Design**
Designer: **Diane Christensen**

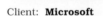

Client: **The Sketching Pad, Inc.**
Design Firm: **The Sketching Pad, Inc.**
Designer: **Barbara Ambrose**

Client: **SunDog**
Design Firm: **Hornall Anderson**
Design Works, Inc.
Designers: **Jack Anderson, David Bates**

Client: **Wentworth Printing Corporation**
Design Firm: **The Adams Group**
Designer: **Ryon Edwards**

Client: **SWIPCO**
Design Firm: **Ross Culbert & Lavery**
Designer: **Peter Ross**

Client: **Analysis & Technology, Inc.**
Design Firm: **Keiler Design Group**
Designer: **Jeff Lin**

Client: **Data Research Associates**
Design Firm: **Phoenix Creative, St. Louis**
Designers: **Eric Thoelke,
Ed Mantels-Seeker**

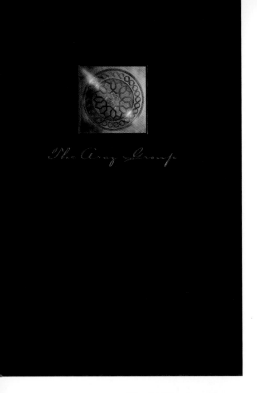

Client: **Neenah Paper**
Design Firm: **Copeland Hirthler design + communications**
Designers: **Brad Copeland, George Hirthler, Melissa James Kimerly,**
Kim Dickinson, Raquel C. Miqueli

Client: **The Araz Group**
Design Firm: **Brad Norr Design**
Designer: **Brad Norr**

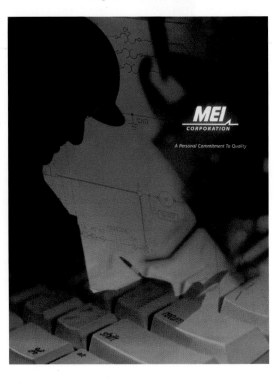

Client: **MEI, Incorporated**
Design Firm: **Design Services, Inc.**
Designers: **Rod Parker, Chris Steiner**

Client: **Starbucks Coffee Company**
Design Firm: **Hornall Anderson Design Works, Inc.**
Designers: **Jack Anderson, Julie Lock,**
Mary Chin Hutchison

Client: **Palm Beach Community College**
Design Firm: **Fisher Graphics**
Designer: **Amy Fisher**

Client: **The California Club**
Design Firm: **The Jefferies Association**
Designers: **Ron Jefferies, Scott Lambert**

Client: **Carpenter & Company, Inc.**
Design Firm: **Korn Design**
Designer: **Denise Korn**

Client: **Elkhorn Construction, Inc.**
Design Firm: **Carter Design, Inc.**
Designers: **Reena Carter, Heidi Domagala**

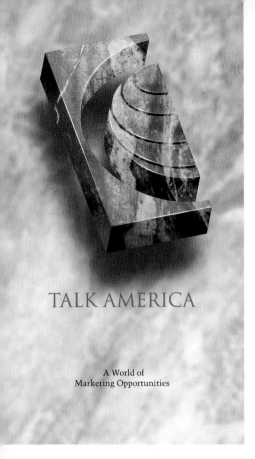

TALK AMERICA

A World of
Marketing Opportunities

Client: **Talk America**
Design Firm: **Imageset**
Designer: **Scott Rowley**

Client: **Airborne Express**
Design Firm: **Hornall Anderson Design Works, Inc.**
Designers: **John Hornall, Lisa Cerveny,
Heidi Favour, Bruce Branson-Meyer**

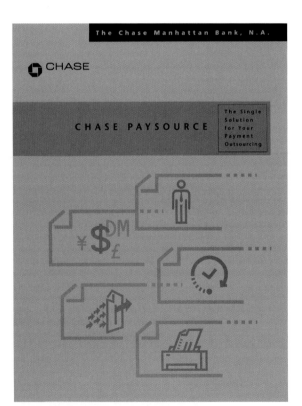

Client: **Chase Manhattan Bank**
Design Firm: **Mike Quon Design Office**
Designer: **Mike Quon**

Client: **GTE VisNet**
Design Firm: **GTE VisNet**
Designers: **Michael Meade, Timothy Bassford**

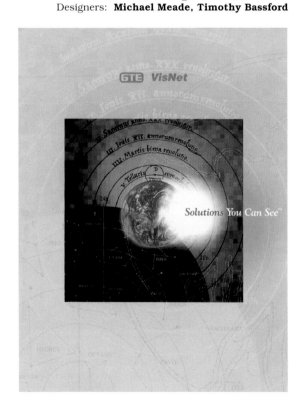

232

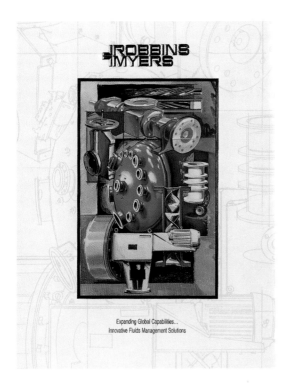

Client: **Indigo Coastal Grill**
Design Firm: **Donahue Studios, Inc.**
Designers: **Andrew Tse,**
Christopher Johnson

Client: **Robbins & Myers, Inc.**
Design Firm: **TDH Marketing & Communications, Inc.**
Designer: **Donna L. Hull**

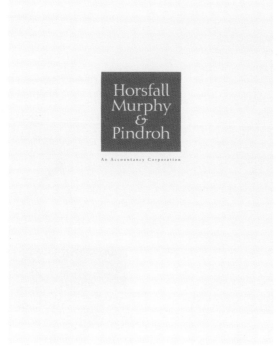

Client: **FHP Health Care**
Design Firm: **Sanft Design, Inc.**
Designers: **Alfred Sanft,**
Paul Howell, David Rengifo

Client: **Horsfall Murphy & Pindroh**
Design Firm: **Dennis S. Juett & Associates, Inc.**
Designers: **Dennis S. Juett, Dennis Scott Juett**

Client: **Teledyne, Inc.**
Design Firm: **The Jefferies Association**
Designers: **Ron Jefferies,**
Troy McQuillen

Client: **GeoCapital**
Design Firm: **Mike Quon Design Office**
Designer: **Mike Quon**

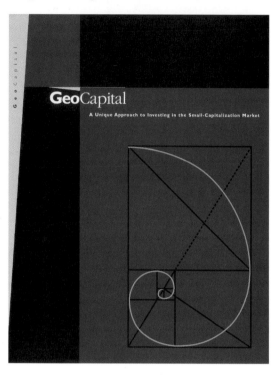

Client: **ABS Worldwide**
Design Firm: **J.S. Design**
Designer: **Jim Shanman**

Client: **Ambrosi & Associates, Inc.**
Design Firm: **Ambrosi & Associates, Inc.**

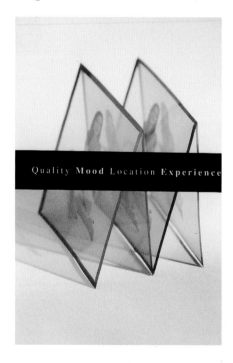

Logos

Client: **Comcast Cablevision Sneak Peek TV**
Design Firm: **ADV Marketing Group, Inc.**
Designer: **Jean-Christian Philippi**

Client: **Autodesk, Inc.**
Design Firm: **Bruce Yelaska Design**
Designer: **Bruce Yelaska**

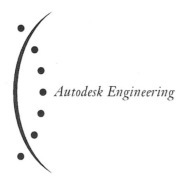

Client: **Jewish Federation of Indianapolis**
Design Firm: **Listenberger Design Assoc.**
Designer: **Richard Listenberger**

Client: **Netstart**
Design Firm: **Elliott Van Deutsch**
Designers: **Erika Maxwell, Rachel Deutsch**

Client: **Marshall Information Service**
Design Firm: **Pollman Marketing Arts, Inc.**
Designers: **Jennifer Pollman, Jennifer Thoren**

Client: **Canon**
Design Firm: **Jager Di Paola Kemp Design**
Designers: **Michael Jager, Cindy Steinberg, Chris Bradley**

Client: **Sonic Restaurants**
Design Firm: **Lippincott & Margulies**
Designers: **Ken Love, Ryan Paul**

Client: **GM-China Technology Institutes**
Design Firm: **General Motors Design**
Designer: **Joann Kallio**

Client: **Cathey Associates, Inc.**
Design Firm: **Cathey Associates, Inc.**
Designer: **Gordon Cathey**

Client: **Tri County Foundation**
Design Firm: **Listenberger Design Assoc.**
Designer: **Richard Listenberger**

Client: **World of New York, Inc.**
Design Firm: **McKnight/Kurland Design**

Client: **American Creative**
Design Firm: **American Creative**
Designers: **Ramon Jaime, Petur Workman**

Client: **Re: Sport**
Design Firm: **Design Marketing**
Designers: **Robert Bettencourt, Jonathan Farley**

Client: **Express Network, Inc.**
Design Firm: **Graphitti Design Group**
Designer: **Holly Logan**

Client: **Center for Housing Resources**
Design Firm: **Cathey Associates, Inc.**
Designer: **Gordon Cathey**

Client: **Vocaltec, Ltd.**
Design Firm: **The Sloan Group**
Designer: **Harriet Goren**

Client: **Designlab**
Design Firm: **Designlab**
Designer: **Kennah Harcum**

Client: **Converse**
Design Firm: **Jager Di Paola Kemp Design**
Designers: **Michael Jager, Janet Johnson, Christopher Vice**

Client: **Copy Craft, Inc.**
Design Firm: **Iconix, Inc.**
Designer: **Kelly J. Schwartz**

Client: **Design Marketing**
Design Firm: **Design Marketing**
Designers: **Robert Bettencourt, Jonathan Farley**

Client: **Georgia State Games Organizing Committee**
Design Firm: **Copeland Hirthler design + communications**
Designers: **Brad Copeland, Kathi Roberts**

Client: **South Press**
Design Firm: **Peterson & Company**
Designer: **Jan Wilson**

237

Client: **Hanes**
Design Firm: **Copeland Hirthler design + communications**
Designers: **Brad Copeland, Michelle Stirna, Raquel C. Migueli**

Client: **Bangkok Dome Plaza**
Design Firm: **FRCH Design Worldwide**
Designers: **Michael Beeghly, Doug Hardenburgh, Shawn Davies, Lisa Proctor**

Client: **Association for the Visually Impaired**
Design Firm: **re: salzman designs**
Designer: **Rick Salzman**

North Country Association for
VISUALLY IMPAIRED

Design Firm: **Copeland Hirthler design + communications**
Designers: **Brad Copeland, Mark Ligameri**

Client: **Common Ground, youth leadership program**
Design Firm: **Keiler Design Group**
Designer: **Jeff Lin**

COMMON GROUND

Client: **Campaign for The Sisters of Mercy and Trocair College**
Design Firm: **Crowley Webb and Associates**
Designer: **Dion Pender**

SupportHope

Client: Finished Art, Inc.
Design Firm: Finished Art, Inc.
Designers: **Kannex Fung, Donna Johnston**

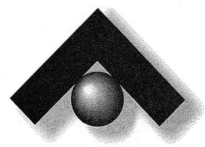

Finished Art inc.

Client: **Tallahassee Tennis Association**
Design Firm: **Synergy Design Group**
Designers: **John LoCastro, Leigh Thompson, Cliff Allen**

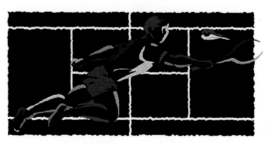

MASTERS CLASSIC
- 1996 -

238

Client: **New York Life and Duke University Hospital**
Design Firm: **Interbrand Schechter**
Designers: **Derek O'Connor, German Castaneda,**
  Gary Stilovich

Client: **Dimon**
Design Firm: **Lippincott & Margulies**
Designers: **Ken Love, Ryan Paul**

Client: **Digital Impact**
Design Firm: **The All-Night Illustration Station**
Designer: **Karen McKee**

Client: **Mega TV**
Design Firm: **Vawter & Vawter**
Designer: **Blake Andujar**

Client: **Church Development Fund, Inc.**
Design Firm: **Hayden Design**
Designer: **Tricia Hayden**

Client: **International Fitness Alliance**
Design Firm: **Freestyle Studio**
Designer: **Rachel Everson Reeser**

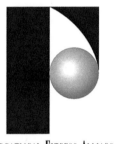

Client: **Second Opinion Interiors**
Design Firm: **Cathey Associates, Inc.**
Designers: **Gordon Cathey, Matt Westapher**

Client: **Clemson University**
Design Firm: **Publications & Marketing Services**
Designers: **David Dryden, Eve Gibson, Steven Serek**

239

Client: **Dayton Mall**
Design Firm: **FRCH Design Worldwide**
Designers: **Michael Beeghly, Charles Aenlle,
Erik Brown, Lori Siebert**

Client: **Audio Technica-U.S., Inc.**
Design Firm: **Babcock & Schmid Associates, Inc.**

Client: **Ecofranchising, Inc.**
Design Firm: **Stephen Loges Graphic Design**
Designer: **Stephen Loges**

Client: **Mac Temps**
Design Firm: **Cipriani Kremer Design**
Designer: **Toni Bowerman**

Client: **Agrium**
Design Firm: **Wendt Advertising**
Designer: **Bob Takeshita**

Client: **Tribek Properties, Inc.**
Design Firm: **Lyerly Agency**
Designer: **Mark Furr**

Client: **Centeon (Armour and Behring)**
Design Firm: **Interbrand Schechter**
Designers: **Gerald Berliner, Janine Bruttin, Wing Chan**

Client: **ServerCom**
Design Firm: **Jack Davis Graphics**
Designer: **Jack W. Davis**

Client: **Chartway**
Design Firm: **Lippincott & Margulies**
Designers: **Connie Birdsall, Gyeong Lee**

Client: **Tenneco**
Design Firm: **Lippincott & Margulies**
Designers: **Ken Love, Jane Bocker**

Client: **Eagle River**
Design Firm: **John Brady Design Consultants**
Designers: **John Brady, Kathy Kendra, Rick Madison**

Client: **International Assessment Network**
Design Firm: **Worrell Design**
Designer: **Karl Peters**

Client: **The Rodeo, electronic prepress studio**
Design Firm: **Spangler Associates**
Designer: **Michael Connors**

Client: **Pediatric Health Care**
Design Firm: **Denise Kemper Design**
Designer: **Denise Stratton Kemper**

Client: **Sir Speedy**
Design Firm: **Design Forum**
Designers: **Scott Smith, Carolyn Zudell**

Client: **Pulte-Harbor Springs**
Design Firm: **Paragraphs Design, Inc.**
Designer: **Michelle Ducayet**

Client: **C. Conde**
Design Firm: **Design Elements, Inc.**
Designer: **Clemente Conde**

Client: **California Center for the Arts Museum**
Design Firm: **Mires Design, Inc.**
Designer: **John Ball**

Client: **DC Interface, Inc.**
Design Firm: **The Kellett Group**
Designers: **Lynn Kertell, Michele Kellett**

Client: **Capehorn International, Inc.**
Design Firm: **66 Communication, Inc.**
Designer: **Chin-Chih Yang**

241

Client: **River Rock Cafe**
Design Firm: **Tackett-Barbaria Design**
Designer: **Patrick Rooney**

Client: **The Praedium Group**
Design Firm: **Skeggs Design**
Designer: **Gary Skeggs**

Client: **Nelson Builders & Consultants**
Design Firm: **Keng's Designs**
Designer: **Robert Keng**

Client: **Young Presidents' Organization for**
Washington University
Design Firm: **Swieter Design United States**
Designers: **Paul Munsterman, John Swieter**

Client: **Acumyn Resource**
Design Firm: **Brad Norr Design**
Designer: **Brad Norr**

Client: **EarthWatch, Inc.**
Design Firm: **Volan Design LLC**
Designers: **Celeste R. Barone, Michele Braverman**

Client: **DeBartolo Properties—Glen Burnie Mall**
Design Firm: **Kiku Obata & Company**
Designer: **Todd Mayberry**

Client: **Motorola, Inc.—LifeSteps**
Design Firm: **ComCorp, Inc.**
Designers: **Deborah Werner, Marc Linne, Jamie Anderson**

242

Client: **West Sound Sports Therapy**
Design Firm: **Swieter Design United States**
Designers: **John Swieter, Jim Vogel**

Client: **Airtouch**
Design Firm: **Addison Seefeld and Brew**
Designer: **John Creson**

Client: **California Center for Pelvic Pain and Fertility**
Design Firm: **Moore Design**
Designer: **Julie Moore**

Client: **Austin Aqua Festival**
Design Firm: **Graphic Edge**
Designer: **Stephanie Phan Roecker**

Client: **Shower Heads Shampoo**
Design Firm: **Swieter Design United States**
Designer: **Paul Munsterman**

Design Firm: **Cassata & Associates**
Designers: **Carl Cassata, James Wolfe**

Client: **Unifications**
Design Firm: **Cathey Associates, Inc.**
Designer: **Gordon Cathey**

Client: **Preview Media**
Design Firm: **Michael Patrick Partners**
Designers: **Bernie Wooster, Laura Dearborn, Roy Tazuma**

Client: **Vail Associates**
Design Firm: **Communication Arts, Inc.**
Designers: **Lynn Williams, Henry Beer**

Client: DSI • **LA**
Design Firm: **Design Services, Inc.**
Designers: **Pat Vining, Carrie Cubler, Anneliese Thornton, Carol Caulfield**

Client: **Renaissance Entertainment Corporation**
Design Firm: **Ellen Bruss Design**
Designers: **Ellen Bruss, Greg Carr, Dae Knight**

Client: **Metropolitan Ballroom & Clubroom**
Design Firm: **Little & Company**
Designers: **Garin Ipsen, Susan Donahue, Tom Riddle, Jim Jackson**

Client: **Matt Rhode, keyboardist-pianist**
Design Firm: **Keiler Design Group**
Designer: **Jeff Lin**

Client: **Erizo Latino**
Design Firm: **Jak Design**
Designer: **Jill Korostoff**

Client: **Little & Company**
Design Firm: **Little & Company**
Designers: **Garin Ipsen, Paul Wharton**

Client: **Aids Council of Northeastern New York**
Design Firm: **re: salzman designs**
Designer: **Rick Salzman**

Client: **The Repair Company**
Design Firm: **Dennis S. Juett & Associates, Inc.**
Designers: **Dennis S. Juett, Dennis Scott Juett**

Client: **Brewed Awakenings**
Design Firm: **Strong Productions**
Designer: **Todd Schatzberg**

Client: **Elder Floridians Foundation**
Design Firm: **Synergy Design Group**
Designer: **John LoCastro**

Client: **Olympic Aid—Atlanta**
Design Firm: **Copeland Hirthler design + communications**
Designers: **Brad Copeland, Todd Brooks**

Client: **Black Creek Golf Club**
Design Firm: **Vawter & Vawter**
Designer: **Carolyn Hunter**

Client: **Idea, Inc.**
Design Firm: **Fire House, Inc.**
Designer: **James A. Hough**

Client: **Monona Terrace Convention Center**
Design Firm: **Corbin Design**
Designers: **Mark Vanderklipp, Jeffry Corbin**

Client: **1996 Atlanta Paralympic Committee**
Design Firm: **Copeland Hirthler design + communications**
Designers: **Brad Copeland, Suzi Miller**

245

Client: **Wireless Financial Services, Inc.**
Design Firm: **Stephen Loges Graphic Design**
Designer: **Stephen Loges**

Client: **Mills Corporation**
Design Firm: **Communication Arts, Inc.**
Designer: **David Dute, Jr.**

Client: **Eagle Rehab Corporation**
Design Firm: **Swieter Design United States**
Designer: **Mark Ford**

Client: **Jet Set Sports**
Design Firm: **Copeland Hirthler design + communications**
Designers: **Brad Copeland, Mark Ligameri**

Client: **Optima, Inc.**
Design Firm: **Jack Weiss Associates**
Designer: **Jack Weiss**

Client: **High Falls Brewing Company**
Design Firm: **McElveney & Palozzi**
   Graphic Design Group, Inc.
Designers: **Steve Palozzi, Matt Nowicki**

Client: **Sports Lab, Inc.**
Design Firm: **Swieter Design United States**
Designer: **John Sweiter**

Client: **Live Picture**
Design Firm: **1185 Design**
Designers: **Julia Foug, Peggy Burke**

Client: **Jack Nicklaus International**
Design Firm: **Copeland Hirthler design + communications**
Designers: **Brad Copeland, Kathi Roberts**

JACK NICKLAUS
INTERNATIONAL GOLF CLUB

Client: **Job Training for Beaver County**
Design Firm: **Sewickley Graphics & Design, Inc.**
Designer: **Sherry Monarko**

Job Training for Beaver County

Client: **Han Dok**
Design Firm: **Lippincott & Margulies**
Designers: **Ken Love, Christiano Andreotti**

Client: **Georgia International Horse Park**
Design Firm: **Copeland Hirthler design + communications**
Designers: **Brad Copeland, Kathi Roberts**

GEORGIA INTERNATIONAL
HORSE PARK

Client: **LINK—school, PTA, student group**
Design Firm: **The Wecker Group**
Designers: **Robert Wecker, Craig Rader**

Client: **Photonic Systems, Inc.**
Design Firm: **Cipriani Kremer Design**
Designers: **Robert Cipriani**

Client: **Photo Graphix—digital photography**
Design Firm: **Out of my Mind Visual Communications**
Designer: **Daniel Knol**

PHOTOGRAPHIX

Client: **Timberform Builders**
Design Firm: **Swieter Design United States**
Designer: **John Sweiter**

Client: **Trinidad Cigar Emporio, Ltd.**
Design Firm: **Shields Design**
Designer: **Charles Shields**

Client: **Delano Regional Medical Center**
Design Firm: **Shields Design**
Designer: **Charles Shields**

Client: **Hands On Greenville**
Design Firm: **Westhouse Design**
Designers: **Daniel Jones, Jack DelGado**

Client: **Red Lobster**
Design Firm: **Lippincott & Margulies**
Designers: **Wayne Van Ver Spoor, Ray Pooleverde**

Client: **Pro Tab**
Design Firm: **Cathey Associates, Inc.**
Designer: **Gordon Cathey**

Client: **Hewlett-Packard—sales builder for Windows**
Design Firm: **Tollner Design Group**
Designer: **Tracy Spenser**

Client: **On the Net**
Design Firm: **Tollner Design Group**
Designer: **Christopher Canote**

Client: **The Green Companies**
Design Firm: **Communication Arts, Inc.**
Designers: **David Dute, Jr., Henry Beer**

248

Client: **Global Guardian**
Design Firm: **Tackett-Barbaria Design**
Designer: **Steve Barbaria**

Global Guardian

Client: **Cybergate Information Services**
Design Firm: **Shields Design**
Designer: **Juan Vega**

CYBERGATE
INFORMATION SERVICES

Client: **Shepherd Center**
Design Firm: **Copeland Hirthler design + communications**
Designers: **Brad Copeland, Melanie Bass**

S H E P H E R D
C E N T E R

A Specialty Hospital

Client: **Meltzer-Martin 6th Anniversary**
Design Firm: **Sullivan Perkins**
Designer: **Brett Baridon**

Client: **Barrington Consulting Group**
Design Firm: **White Design, Inc.**
Designers: **John White, Aram Youssefian**

Client: **Club Mavericks—Dallas Mavericks**
Design Firm: **Swieter Design United States**
Designer: **Julie Poth**

Client: **Los Angeles Ice Dogs**
Design Firm: **J.S. Design**
Designer: **Jim Shanman**

Client: **Riverwood**
Design Firm: **Copeland Hirthler design + communications**
Designers: **Brad Copeland, Todd Brooks**

Client: **Daka International**
Design Firm: **Fitch, Inc.**
Designers: **Robert Wood, Julie D'Andrea, Ellen Hartshorne**

Client: **Vanguard Airlines**
Design Firm: **Matrix International Assoc.**
Designers: **Duane Wiens, Carl Baden**

Client: **Rockingham Council of the Arts, Inc.**
Design Firm: **Seran Design**
Designer: **Sang Yoon**

Client: **Street Savage**
Design Firm: **Swieter Design United States**
Designer: **Mark Ford**

Client: **PrintCom**
Design Firm: **Uppercase Design**
Designer: **Justin Deister**

Client: **Corning Enterprises—Festival of Art**
Design Firm: **Michael Orr + Associates, Inc.**
Designers: **Michael R. Orr, Thomas Freeland**

Client: **Shaw's "Fresh Ideas" Magazine**
Design Firm: **re: salzman designs**
Designer: **Rick Salzman**

Client: **The Iams Company**
Design Firm: **Seta Appleman & Showell**
Designer: **Jeff Fulwiler**

250

Client: **FEAT**
Design Firm: **Tackett-Barbaria Design**
Designer: **Pam Matsuda**

F E A T
*Families For Early
Autism Treatment*

Client: **Lucas County Children Services**
Design Firm: **Orwig Communications**
Designers: **Ken Orwig, Julia Orwig**

One Church.
One Child.

An
African-American
tradition.

Client: **Southern California Edison/Edison International**
Design Firm: **Addison Seefeld and Brew**
Designers: **Micaela Merce, Creighton Dinsmore**

SOUTHERN CALIFORNIA
EDISON

An *EDISON INTERNATIONAL* Company

Client: **Dr. Hook-Up**
Design Firm: **Graphitti Design Group**
Designer: **Orlando Abrey**

Client: **Chili Beer Cantina**
Design Firm: **Tieken Design & Creative Services**
Designers: **Fred E. Tieken, Tad A. Smith**

Client: **Hospice of the North Country**
Design Firm: **re: salzman designs**
Designer: **Rick Salzman**

Client: **Addison-Wesley Publishing Company**
Design Firm: **Watts Design? Inc.**
Designer: **Michael Boland**

Client: **Ackerberg Group**
Design Firm: **Tilka Design**
Designers: **Jane Tilka, Carla Mueller, Mark Mularz**

Client: **TriStar Airlines**
Design Firm: **Tusk Studios**
Designer: **Debra Heiser**

Client: **Paramount Pictures—Constellation Films**
Design Firm: **Tim Girvin Design, Inc.**
Designer: **Tim Girvin**

CONSTELLATION FILMS

Client: **Hot Stuff, Inc.**
Design Firm: **Wild Garlic Art Studio**
Designer: **Zbigniew Jastrzebski**

Client: **Ignition**
Design Firm: **Swieter Design United States**
Designers: **John Swieter, Mark Ford**

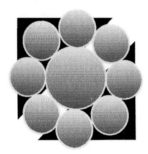

Client: **MLink Technologies, Inc.**
Design Firm: **Hayden Design**
Designer: **Tricia Hayden**

Client: **Motorola, Inc.—Motorola Assist**
Design Firm: **ComCorp, Inc.**
Designers: **Deborah Werner, Jamie Anderson**

Client: **Taylor Subscription Talk**
Design Firm: **Striegel and Associates**
Designers: **Peggy Striegel, Tom Schmeltz, Phil Cooper**

Client: **The Bose Corporation**
Design Firm: **Cipriani Kremer Design**
Designer: **Robert Cipriani**

Client: **The McGraw-Hill Companies**
Design Firm: **Lippincott & Margulies**
Designers: **Connie Birdsall, Jane Ashley**

Client: **Prism Venture Partners**
Design Firm: **Tom Davis + Company**
Designers: **Way Tay, Tom Davis**

The McGraw·Hill Companies

Client: **Larsen Interactive**
Design Firm: **Larsen Design Office, Inc.**
Designers: **Marc Kundmann, Sean McKay**

Design Firm: **AmQuest Financial Corporation**
Design Firm: **Matrix International Assoc.**
Designers: **Duane Wiens, Carl Baden**

Client: **China-America Technology Investment Group, Inc.**
Design Firm: **Hayden Design**
Designer: **Tricia Hayden**

Client: **ReliaStar Corporation**
Design Firm: **Larsen Design Office, Inc.**
Designer: **Marc Kundmann**

RELIASTAR

Client: **HealthSystem Minnesota**
Design Firm: **Larsen Design Office, Inc.**
Designers: **Larsen Design Staff**

Client: **Kids Row, Inc.**
Design Firm: **Sheilini Singh**
Designer: **Sheilini Singh**

Client: **Ascent Entertainment**
Design Firm: **The Graphic Expression, Inc.**
Designer: **Kurt Finkbeiner**

Client: **Snelling Personnel Services**
Design Firm: **Duncan/Day Advertising**
Designer: **Stacey Day**

253

Client: **Tenet**
Design Firm: **Addison Seefeld and Brew**
Designers: **John Creson, Karen Smidth**

Client: **LG (Lucky Goldstar)**
Design Firm: **Landor Associates**
Designers: **Rachel Wear, Courtney Reeser,
Margaret Youngblood**

Client: **Netscape**
Design Firm: **Landor Associates**
Designers: **Judy Hemming, Courtney Reeser,
Margaret Youngblood**

NETSCAPE

Client: **Cygnus Therapeutic Systems**
Design Firm: **Landor Associates**
Designers: **Rachel Wear, Judy Hemming, Courtney Reeser,
Margaret Youngblood**

CYGNUS

Client: **California Community Foundation**
Design Firm: **Bright & Associates**
Designer: **Ray Wood**

CALIFORNIA COMMUNITY
FOUNDATION

Client: **Osmonics**
Design Firm: **Larsen Design Office, Inc.**
Designer: **Sascha Boecker**

Client: **Los Angeles Convention & Visitors Bureau**
Design Firm: **Bright & Associates**
Designers: **Taleen Bedikian, Ray Wood, Keith Bright**

LOS ANGELES
Convention & Visitors Bureau

Client: **Sky's the Limit**
Design Firm: **Antista Fairclough Design**
Designers: **Tom Antista, Thomas Fairclough**

Client: **Young At Art**
Design Firm: **The Graphic Expression, Inc.**
Designer: **Kurt Finkbeiner**

Client: **Landmark Graphics Corporation**
Design Firm: **Savage Design Group**
Designer: **Tom Hair**

Client: **Northeast Health Systems**
Design Firm: **Tom Davis + Company**
Designer: **Tom Davis**

Client: **Chesapeake Bagel Bakery**
Design Firm: **Kiku Obata & Company**
Designer: **Jane McNeely**

Client: **National Physician's Network**
Design Firm: **Antista Fairclough Design**
Designers: **Tom Antista, Thomas Fairclough**

Client: **Keycorp**
Design Firm: **Landor Associates**
Designers: **Jennifer Bostic, Courtney Reeser, Margaret Youngblood**

Client: **Chesebrough-Pond's**
Design Firm: **Hans Flink Design, Inc.**
Designers: **Hans Flink, Chang Mei Lin, Mark Knickonis**

Client: **Bayer Corporation**
Design Firm: **Hans Flink Design, Inc.**
Designers: **Hans D. Flink, Suzanne Clark**

Client: **Buffalo State College Performing Arts Center**
Design Firm: **Crowley Webb and Associates**
Designer: **Rob Wynne**

Client: **Mercury Marine**
Design Firm: **Bright & Associates**
Designer: **Ray Wood**

Client: **Step & Stride**
Design Firm: **DiSanto Design**
Designer: **Roseanne DiSanto**

Client: **Mills Corporation**
Design Firm: **Communication Arts, Inc.**
Designer: **David Dute, Jr.**

Client: **Procter & Gamble**
Design Firm: **Hans Flink Design, Inc.**
Designer: **Hans Flink**

Client: **Apria Healthcare**
Design Firm: **Landor Associates**
Designers: **Denise Goldman, Grant Peterson, Courtney Reeser, Margaret Youngblood**

Client: **St. Tammany Humane Society**
Design Firm: **Design Services, Inc.**
Designers: **Rod Parker, Todd Palisi**

Client: **Friedman, Billings, Ramsey & Co., Inc.**
Design Firm: **The Invisions Group Ltd.**
Designers: **John Cabot Lodge, Denise Sparhawk**

Client: **Icicle Seafoods, Inc.**
Design Firm: **Faine/Oller Productions, Inc.**
Designers: **Catherine Oller, Nancy Stentz, Martin French**

Client: **National Gay & Lesbian Task Force**
Design Firm: **Hershey Associates**
Designer: **R. Christine Hershey**

Client: **New York State Electric & Gas**
Design Firm: **Michael Orr + Associates, Inc.**
Designers: **Michael R. Orr, Thomas Freeland**

Client: **Princeton Financial Systems**
Design Firm: **Cook and Shanosky Associates, Inc.**
Designers: **Roger Cook, Keith Testa**

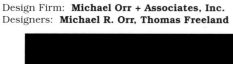

Client: **Time Warner Dreamshop**
Design Firm: **Frankfurt Balkind Partners**
Designers: **Kent Hunter, Aubrey Balkind, Arturo Aranda**

Client: **Michael's Restaurant**
Design Firm: **The Wecker Group**
Designers: **Robert Wecker, Ruth Minerva, Craig Rader**

Client: **Textures of Africa**
Design Firm: **Ledom + Pollock Advertising + Design**
Designer: **Neil Pollock**

Client: **KC's Coffee**
Design Firm: **Listenberger Design Assoc.**
Designer: **Richard Listenberger**

257

Client: **Theis • Doolittle Associates, Inc.**
Design Firm: **EAT, Incorporated**
Designers: **Patrice Eilts-Jobe, Toni O'Bryan**

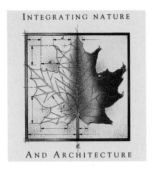

Client: **Cool Beans Café**
Design Firm: **Phoenix Creative, St. Louis**
Designer: **Kathy Wilkinson**

Client: **Daytons**
Design Firm: **Minneapolis Design Company**
Designer: **Robert Warren Carlson**

Client: **Consolite Corporation Boat Signage Division**
Design Firm: **Tracy Sabin Graphic Design**
Designer: **Tracy Sabin**

Client: **Shandwick USA**
Design Firm: **Phoenix Creative, St. Louis**
Designer: **Steve Brenner**

Client: **Cranford Street**
Design Firm: **Mires Design**
Designers: **Tracy Sabin, José Serrano**

Client: **The Church of Today**
Design Firm: **Mires Design, Inc.**
Designers: **José Serrano, Toni MacCabe**

Client: **Har Mar**
Design Firm: **Minneapolis Design Company**
Designer: **Robert Warren Carlson**

258

Client: **Harcourt Brace Jovanovich**
Design Firm: **Mires Design**
Designers: **Tracy Sabin, José Serrano**

Client: **The Hayes Co., Inc.**
Design Firm: **Love Packaging Group**
Designer: **Tracy Holdeman**

Client: **BB Interactive—Blair Beebe**
Design Firm: **Cawrse & Effect**
Designer: **Andrew Cawrse**

Client: **Pioneer**
Design Firm: **Imagicians Ad & PR**
Designer: **Jim Rosanio, Jr.**

Client: **Roy Rogers**
Design Firm: **King Casey**
Designers: **John Chrzanowski, Christen Kucharik**

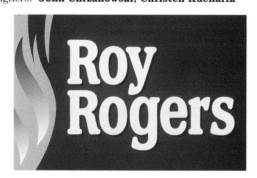

Client: **Nickelodeon**
Design Firm: **Harrisberger Creative**
Designer: **Lynn Harrisberger**

Client: **Swix Sport**
Design Firm: **OMNI Studio**
Designer: **Jerry Choat**

Client: **Lambert Design Studio**
Design Firm: **Lambert Design Studio**
Designer: **Joy Cathey Price**

Client: **The Magellan Group**
Design Firm: **Primary Design, Inc.**
Designer: **Christine Hardiman**

Client: **Paramount's Kings Island**
Design Firm: **Visual Marketing Associates**
Designer: **Gregory Vennerholm**

Client: **Nike, Deion Sanders Shoe Line**
Design Firm: **Mires Design**
Designers: **Tracy Sabin, José Serrano**

Client: **St. Paul's Episcopal Day School**
Design Firm: **EAT, Incorporated**
Designers: **Patrice A.M. Eilts-Jobe, Kevin Tracy**

Client: **Tratt-O-Ria Della Via Restaurant**
Design Firm: **McDill Design**
Designers: **Kris Kelly, Michael Dillon**

Client: **MedPro, Inc.**
Design Firm: **Design Elements, Inc.**
Designer: **Clemente Conde**

Client: **Chukar Cherries**
Design Firm: **Walsh and Associates, Inc.**
Designer: **Miriam Lisco**

Client: **The Hahn Company Web Site**
Design Firm: **Tracy Sabin Graphic Design**
Designer: **Tracy Sabin**

260

Client: **Fyshsandwych**
Design Firm: **Next Year's News, Inc.**
Designers: **Dwight Ashley, Chris Hoffman**

Client: **Endless Summer**
Design Firm: **Bailey Design Group**
Designer: **Steve Perry**

Client: **The Oaks Shopping Center**
Design Firm: **Talbot Design Group**
Designers: **Chris Kosman, Gaylyn Talbot**

Client: **The Hayes Co., Inc.—Sweet Pea Garden**
Design Firm: **Love Packaging Group**
Designer: **Tracy Holdeman**

Client: **Total Quality Apparel Resource**
Design Firm: **Mike Brower**
Designers: **Mike Brower, Tracy Sabin**

Client: **Campiello**
Design Firm: **Little & Company**
Designers: **Kathy Soranno, Jim Jackson**

Client: **Hannaford Bros. Company**
Design Firm: **Gerstman+Meyers, Inc.**
Designer: **Susan Payne**

Client: **NBC Desktop Video**
Design Firm: **Hadtke Design**
Designers: **Richard Karsten, Cindy Martinez**

261

Client: **The Moseley Corporation**
Design Firm: **Malcolm Grear Designers, Inc.**

Client: **Afrex Int.**
Design Firm: **King Casey**
Designers: **John Chrzanowski, Amy Cepolla**

Client: **International Assessment Network**
Design Firm: **Worrell Design**
Designer: **Karl Peters**

Client: **Pompano Square**
Design Firm: **Mall Olcon Marketing Group**
Designer: **Tracy Sabin**

Client: **SkiView**
Design Firm: **John Brady Design Consultants**
Designers: **John Brady, Kathy Kendra, Rick Madison**

Client: **Triangle Internet Company**
Design Firm: **Image Associates, Inc.**
Designer: **Leigh-Erin M. Salmon**

Client: **Chief Executive Magazine**
Design Firm: **Tracy Sabin Graphic Design**
Designer: **Tracy Sabin**

Client: **Calypso Software Systems**
Design Firm: **Tracy Sabin Graphic Design**
Designer: **Tracy Sabin**

Client: **SeaVision**
Design Firm: **John Brady Design Consultants**
Designers: **John Brady, Rick Madison**

Client: **Chaos Lures**
Design Firm: **Mires Design**
Designers: **Tracy Sabin, José Serrano**

Client: **Swix Sport**
Design Firm: **OMNI Studio**
Designer: **Jerry Choat**

Client: **Fruit of the Loom**
Design Firm: **Gerstman+Meyers, Inc.**
Designer: **Diane Sheridan**

Client: **X-Century Studios**
Design Firm: **Shimokochi/Reeves**
Designers: **Mamoru Shimokochi, Anne Reeves**

Client: **Fireflies Program**
Design Firm: **Sackett Design Associates**
Designers: **Mark Sackett, Wayne Sokomoto, James Sokomoto**

Client: **Leaf & Ladle**
Design Firm: **Minneapolis Design Company**
Designer: **Robert Warren Carlson**

Client: **Denny's Restaurants**
Design Firm: **King Casey, Inc.**
Designer: **John Chrzanowski**

Client: **Ralcorp Holdings**
Design Firm: **Gerstman+Meyers, Inc.**
Designer: **Monica Kurkemelis**

Client: Hallmark Entertainment
Design Firm: **Frankfurt Balkind Partners**
Designers: **Kent Hunter, Aubrey Balkind, Christopher Yin, Stephen Hutchinson**

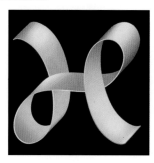

Client: **San Diego Gas & Electric**
Design Firm: **Franklin Stoorza**
Designers: **Tracy Sabin, Craig Fuller**

Client: **Rendition**
Design Firm: **Mortensen Design**
Designer: **Gordon Mortensen**

Client: **Novell, Inc.**
Design Firm: **Frankfurt Balkind Partners**
Designers: **Kent Hunter, Aubrey Balkind, Kin Yuen**

Client: **Jun Hwa Development Co., Ltd.**
Design Firm: **66 Communication, Inc.**
Designer: **Chin-Chih Yang**

Client: **McDill Design**
Design Firm: **McDill Design**
Designers: **Michael Dillon, Joel Harmeling**

Client: **Boston Museum of Science**
Design Firm: **BrandEquity International**
Designer: **Joseph Selame**

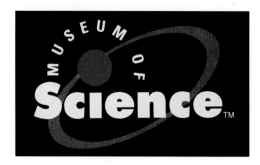

Client: **MB Focus Weight, Inc.**
Design Firm: **O&J Design, Inc,**
Designer: **Inhi Clara Kim**

Client: **DuPont**
Design Firm: **The Madison Group**
Designer: **Yoshifumi Fujii**

Client: **ICI Polyurethanes**
Design Firm: **Robert Michael Communications, Inc.**
Designers: **Robert M. Colleluori, Kate Humes, Denise Fells**

Client: **Rimage Corporation**
Design Firm: **Worrell Design**
Designer: **Kasey Worrell**

Client: **HOK Architects**
Design Firm: **Phoenix Creative, St. Louis**
Designer: **Deborah Finkelstein**

Client: **Young Imaginations**
Design Firm: **Sackett Design Associates**
Designer: **Mark Sackett**

Client: **Lakemary Center**
Design Firm: **EAT, Incorporated**
Designers: **Patrice Eilts-Jobe, Toni O'Bryan**

Client: **Lower Colorado River Authority**
Design Firm: **Tocquigny Advertising and Design**
Designers: **Kelley Cain, David Martino**

265

Client: **TV America**
Design Firm: **O&J Design, Inc.**
Designer: **Andrzej J. Olejniczak**

Client: **Schwarz**
Design Firm: **Waln Communications Group**
Designers: **Bill Concannon, Hollis Morgan**

Client: **US Assist**
Design Firm: **Degnen Associates, Inc.**
Designers: **Stephen Degnen, David Fowler**

Client: **Mervyn's**
Design Firm: **Sackett Design Associates**
Designers: **Mark Sackett, Wayne Sokomoto, James Sokomoto**

Client: **Interex**
Design Firm: **Insight**
Designers: **Tracy Holdeman, Sherrie Holdeman**

Client: **Total Noral Imaging**
Design Firm: **Waln Communications Group**
Designers: **Bill Concannon, Hollis Morgan**

Client: **Pulte Home Corporation of Massachusetts**
Design Firm: **Primary Design, Inc.**
Designer: **Revelle Taillon**

Client: **Arizona State University,
    College of Achitecture & Environmental Design**
Design Firm: **Sanft Design, Inc.**
Designers: **Alfred Sanft, Paul Howell, David Rengifo**

Client: **Gtech Corporation**
Design Firm: **Chapman and Partners**
Designer: **David Chapman**

Client: **Big Weenie Records**
Design Firm: **Tracy Sabin Graphic Design**
Designer: **Tracy Sabin**

Client: **Telecel**
Design Firm: **King Casey, Inc.**
Designers: **John Chrzanowski, Steve Brent**

Client: **DuPont—Lycra**
Design Firm: **The Madison Group**
Designer: **Yoshifumi Fujii**

Client: **Charlotte Russe**
Design Firm: **Tracy Sabin Graphic Design**
Designer: **Tracy Sabin**

Client: **Pulte-Sierra Ridge**
Design Firm: **Paragraphs Design, Inc.**
Designer: **Kelli Evans**

Client: **3COM—Baseball & Football Stadium**
Design Firm: **Clement Mok Designs**
Designers: **Andrew Cawrse, Mark Crumpacker**

Client: **Pulte-Regatta**
Design Firm: **Paragraphs Design, Inc.**
Designer: **Michelle Ducayet**

Client: **Glenbrook Square**
Design Firm: **Gibson Communication Group, Inc.**
Designer: **Chuck Snider**

Client: **International Commission on Irrigation and Drainage**
Design Firm: **Carter Design, Inc.**
Designers: **Reena Carter, Jim Carter**

Client: **GEARBOX interactive**
Design Firm: **Poillucci Design Group**
Designer: **Anthony Poillucci**

Client: **Passarelli and Fascia**
Design Firm: **Mastrogiannis Design, Inc.**
Designers: **Peter Mastrogiannis, Chip Balch**

Client: **Population Reference Bureau, Inc.**
Design Firm: **Dever Designs, Inc.**
Designer: **Jeffrey L. Dever**

Client: **Mediabridge, Inc.**
Design Firm: **Edward Walter Design, Inc.**
Designer: **Edward Walter**

Client: **Friends of Lorenzo**
Design Firm: **Jowaisas Design**
Designer: **Elizabeth Jowaisas**

Client: **Pragmatics**
Design Firm: **Edward Walter Design, Inc.**
Designer: **Edward Walter**

Client: **MacTemps (Portfolio)**
Design Firm: **Cipriani Kremer Design**
Designer: **Toni Bowerman**

Client: **Hotel Kinzan**
Design Firm: **Profile Design**
Designers: **Kenichi Nishiwaki, Jun Kidokoro**

KARAOKE LOUNGE

Client: **Northeast Health Care Quality Foundation**
Design Firm: **Jasper & Bridge Associates**
Designer: **Bob Bettencourt**

Northeast Health Care Quality Foundation

Client: **MedAcoustics, Inc.**
Design Firm: **Casper Design Group**
Designers: **Charlene Tiani, Anderson Gin**

MedAcoustics

Client: **The Belden Brick Company**
Design Firm: **Identity Center**
Designers: **Wayne Kosterman, Darin Hasley**

BELDEN

Client: **Duo Delights**
Design Firm: **Lambert Design Studio**
Designer: **Joy Cathey Price**

Sweet Sinsations

Design Firm: **Briggs & Briggs**
Design Firm: **Richland Design Assoicates**
Designer: **Tim Preston**

B R I G G S   B R I G G S

Client: **Expersoft Corporation**
Design Firm: **Abrams Design Group**
Designer: **Kim Ferrell**

EXPERSOFT

Client: **The Gabriel Consortium, Inc.**
Design Firm: **Dever Design, Inc.**
Designer: **Jeff Dever**

the GABRIEL Consortium, inc.

Client: **Strategy**
Design Firm: **Profile Design**
Designers: **Kenichi Nishiwaki, Jeanne Namkung**

STRATEGY

Client: **Firefox Industries**
Design Firm: **Elias/Savion Advertising**
Designer: **Ronnie Savion**

Client: **MIDCOM**
Design Firm: **Hornall Anderson Design Works, Inc.**
Designers: **John Hornall, Jana Nishi, David Bates**

Client: **Black Hawk Resources**
Design Firm: **Advertising Design, Inc.**
Designer: **Eric Finstad**

Design Firm: **Columbia 300 International**
Design Firm: **Eickhoff Hannan Rue**
Designer: **Mark A. Rue**

Client: **ScanAm Group**
Design Firm: **Galen Design Associates**
Designer: **Larry Galen Larson**

Client: **Nextlink**
Design Firm: **Hornall Anderson Design Works, Inc.**
Designers: **Jack Anderson, Mary Hermes, David Bates, Mary Chin Hutchison**

Client: **Aronoff Center**
Design Firm: **FRCH Design Worldwide**
Designers: **Michael Beeghly, Martin Treu, Eric Daniel**

Client: **Landquisitions, Inc.**
Design Firm: **Grizzell & Co.**
Designer: **John H. Grizzell**

Client: **Executives of Texas Homes for Children**
Design Firm: **Capt. Flynn Advertising**
Designer: **Tom Rigsby**

Client: **OPASTCO**
Design Firm: **Coleman Design Group**
Designers: **John Coleman, Amanda Grupe**

Client: **Odessa Design**
Design Firm: **AGdesign**
Designer: **Amanda Grupe**

Client: **Motiva Software**
Design Firm: **Laura Coe Design Associates**
Designers: **Ryoichi Yotsumoto, Laura Coe Wright**

Client: **Rovar Soaps**
Design Firm: **McNulty & Co.**
Designers: **Jennifer McNulty, Ben Lopez**

Design Firm: **Skagit Symphony**
Design Firm: **Galen Design Associates**
Designer: **Larry Galen Larson**

Client: **PG&E Enterprise—Vantus**
Design Firm: **Lisa Levin Design**
Designers: **Lisa Levin, Sam Lising**

Client: **InterAlliance, Inc.**
Design Firm: **Philip Quinn & Partners**
Designer: **Philip Quinn**

Client: **d-tec Corporation—Chemgard division**
Design Firm: **Adam Filippo & Associates**
Designer: **David Christian Zimmerly**

Client: **New York New Media Association**
Design Firm: **Edward Walter Design, Inc.**
Designer: **Martin Brynell**

Client: **Fletcher, Harkness, Cohen, Moneyhun, Inc.**
Design Firm: **Richland Design Associates**
Designer: **Tim Preston**

FLETCHER HARKNESS COHEN MONEYHUN, INC.

Client: **BBN Planet**
Design Firm: **Barrett Communications, Inc.**
Designer: **Nadine Flowers**

Client: **Aerea**
Design Firm: **Lawrence Design Group, Inc.**
Designer: **Marie-Christine Lawrence**

Client: **Identigene Paternity Testing**
Design Firm: **Goldsmith/Jeffrey**
Designer: **Dean Hacohen**

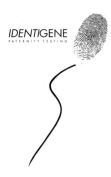

Client: **Mezcal Importers, Inc.**
Design Firm: **Banks & Associates**
Designer: **Lionel Banks**

Client: **Grand View Golf Club**
Design Firm: **Seman Design Group**
Designer: **Richard M. Seman**

Client: **Mediaweek Magazine**
Design Firm: **Adweek Magazines Promotion
Art Department**
Designer: **Katherine Machado**

Client: **Metricom**
Design Firm: **Hausman Design**
Designer: **Stephen Turner**

Client: **Hamilton County (Ohio)
Environmental Priorities Project**
Design Firm: **Shandwick USA**
Designer: **Phillip Booth**

Client: **Hawaii OnLine**
Design Firm: **Hawaii OnLine**
Designer: **Keith Sasaki**

Client: **Genex Cooperative, Inc.**
Design Firm: **Saatchi & Saatchi Business Communications**
Designer: **Susan Murphy McGuane**

Client: **Karisi Communications: Africa Online**
Design Firm: **Richland Design Associates**
Designer: **Tim Preston**

Client: **Microxperts Computer**
Design Firm: **Watt, Roop & Co.**
Designer: **Kurt R. Roscoe**

Client: **J.P.I.**
Design Firm: **VWA Group, Inc.**
Designer: **Tabitha Bogard**

Client: **AIM USA**
Design Firm: **Elias/Savion Advertising**
Designer: **Ronnie Savon**

Client: **Accents Hardware**
Design Firm: **Goodson + Yu Design, Ltd.**
Designers: **Roger Yu, Carole Goodson**

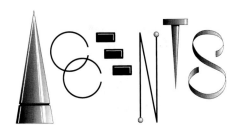

Client: **Ace Commercial, Inc.**
Design Firm: **Zenn Graphic Design**
Designer: **Zengo Yoshida**

Client: **Credit Union 1**
Design Firm: **Bombek**
Designer: **Carey Kimura**

273

Client: **Event Design**
Design Firm: **The Weller Institute for the Cure of Design, Inc.**
Designer: **Don Weller**

E V E N T   D E S I G N

Client: **MCEN—cultural arts exchange program**
Design Firm: **Rassman Design**
Designers: **Lyn D'Amato, John Rassman, Amy Rassman**

MultiCultural Events Network

Client: **Philadelphia Chamber Music Society**
Design Firm: **Randi Margrabia Design**
Designer: **Randi Shalit Margrabia**

10TH ANNIVERSARY SEASON
— PHILADELPHIA —
CHAMBER MUSIC SOCIETY

Client: **Primadonna Casino Resorts**
Design Firm: **Concept Marketing Design**
Designer: **Reg Avey**

PRIMADONNA
Resorts, Inc.

Client: **Network MCI Services**
Design Firm: **Coleman Design Group**
Designers: **Steve Alexander, John Coleman**

LANS ASAP

Client: **Miami Valley Economic Development Coalition**
Design Firm: **Edward Howard & Co.**
Designer: **Bob Kelemen**

MIAMI VALLEY
Economic Development Coalition

Client: **Onboard Media**
Design Firm: **Axioma, Inc.**
Designer: **José Bila Rodriguez**

onboard
M E D I A

Client: **Spectrum Consulting Group, Inc.**
Design Firm: **Edward Howard & Co.**
Designer: **Bob Kelemen**

Spectrum
Consulting
Group, Inc.

Client: **CD-R Solutions**
Design Firm: **Monteverde Advertising & Design**
Designer: **Larry Monteverde**

Client: **ALPHARMA**
Design Firm: **Corporate Branding Partnership**
Designers: **Michael Glass, Jim Gregory**

Client: **Jameson Health System**
Design Firm: **Adam Filippo & Associates**
Designer: **Barbara Peak Long**

Client: **Colony Metal**
Design Firm: **Unit One, Inc.**
Designers: **Unit One, Inc.**

Client: **Horizon Hospital System**
Design Firm: **Bradley Brown Design Group, Inc.**
Designer: **Robert Kiernan**

Client: **Disclosure, Inc.**
Design Firm: **Lomangino Studio, Inc.**
Designer: **Kim Pollack**

Client: **Insurance Information Technologies**
Design Firm: **Roman Design**
Designer: **Lisa Romanowski**

Client: **The Hamptons International Film Festival**
Design Firm: **Art O Mat Design**
Designers: **Jacki McCarthy, Mark Kaufman**

Client: **Blue Chip Financial Management, LP.**
Design Firm: **HC Design**
Designers: **Howard Clare, Chuck Sundin**

Client: **St. James Sales & Consulting Group, Ltd.**
Design Firm: **Evolution Communications**
Designer: **Pat Noonan-Hastings**

Client: **Thorp Music**
Design Firm: **Crossover Graphics**
Designer: **Donald Bullach**

Client: **Digital Delivery**
Design Firm: **Gill Fishman Assocs., Inc.**
Designers: **Gill Fishman, Michael Persons**

Client: **COMSAT, Planet 1**
Design Firm: **HC Design**
Designers: **Howard Clare, Chuck Sundin**

PLANET 1^{SM}

Client: **Checchi**
Design Firm: **Dever Designs, Inc.**
Designer: **Jeffrey L. Dever**

CHECCHI

Client: **Perigis—software for geographic information**
Design Firm: **Rassman Design**
Designers: **John Rassman, Amy Rassman**

PERIGIS

Client: **Microsoft Corporation**
Design Firm: **Hornall Anderson Design Works, Inc.**
Designers: **Jack Anderson, John Anicker,
Mary Chin Hutchison**

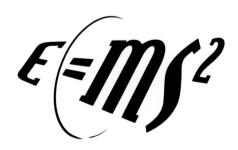

Client: **Summit Strategies, Inc.**
Design Firm: **McDermott Design**
Designer: **Bill McDermott**

Client: **Sudden Impact Auto Rebuilders**
Design Firm: **Bullet Communications, Inc.**
Designer: **Tim Scott**

Client: **Business Systems Online, Inc.**
Design Firm: **Cosaro and Associates**
Designer: **Rick A. Cosaro**

Client: **Colorado Asphalt Pavement Association**
Design Firm: **Unit One, Inc.**
Designers: **Unit One, Inc.**

Client: **Allen Engineering**
Design Firm: **Turner Design**
Designer: **Bert Turner**

Client: **Rock Creek Technologies**
Design Firm: **Axis Communications**
Designer: **Chris Paul, Craig Byers**

Client: **Bellin Hospital/Bellin Heartwatch Plus**
Design Firm: **Bellin Hospital Communications Dept.**
Designer: **Daniel Green**

Client: **Future South Development Corp.**
Design Firm: **McDermott Design**
Designer: **Bill McDermott**

Client: **J.L. Alexander Group**
Design Firm: **LaFond Design**
Designer: **Lori LaFond LaMore**

Client: **Autosafe**
Design Firm: **Vince Rini Design**
Designer: **Vince Rini**

Client: **Distributive Data Systems**
Design Firm: **Doyle Robinson Advertising/Design**
Designer: **Doyle Robinson**

Client: **Database**
Design Firm: **Jasper & Bridge Associates**
Designer: Ken Hallee

Client: **St. Clair Hospital**
Design Firm: **Bradley Brown Design Group, Inc.**
Designer: **Robert Kiernan**

Client: **QTE Systems**
Design Firm: **McKnight/Kurland Design**

Client: **Q-Matrix**
Design Firm: **Rick Jackson**
Designers: **Rick Jackson, Dean Del Sesto**

Client: **Quality, Inc.**
Design Firm: **Gill Fishman Assoc., Inc.**
Designers: **Spencer Ladd, Gill Fishman**

278

Client: **Saint Luke's Episcopal Church**
Design Firm: **The Weller Institute for the Cure of Design, Inc.**
Designer: **Don Weller**

Client: **Whisper Homes & Construction**
Design Firm: **Genuine Graphics**
Designer: **Mike Virosteck**

Client: **White Arts Printing**
Design Firm: **Indiana Design Consortium**

Client: **Women in Development of Greater Boston**
Design Firm: **Korn Design**
Designer: **Denise Korn**

Client: **The Bike Rack**
Design Firm: **Joseph Dieter Visual Communications**
Designer: **Joseph M. Dieter, Jr.**

Client: **Streamline Graphics**
Design Firm: **Evenson Design Group**
Designer: **Glenn Sakamoto**

Client: **Western Vitamin Roundtable**
Design Firm: **Dennis S. Juett & Associates, Inc.**
Designers: **Dennis S. Juett, Dennis Scott Juett**

Client: **San Francisco Opera Guild**
Design Firm: **Profile Design**
Designers: **Kenichi Nishiwaki, Lena Tonseth**

279

Client: **Crossover Project**
Design Firm: **Rassman Design**
Designers: **Lyn D'Amato, John Rassman, Amy Rassman**

CROSSOVER PROJECT

Client: **Art Therapy Institute of San Franciso**
Design Firm: **Debra Lamfers Design**
Designer: **Debra Lamfers**

Art Therapy Institute
OF SAN FRANCISCO

Client: **PRAIXS**
Design Firm: **The Weller Institute for the Cure of Design, Inc.**
Designer: **Don Weller**

P R A I X S

Client: **Bone Health Diagnostics**
Design Firm: **Kyle Design**
Designer: **Cathy Jones Kyle**

Bone Health
Diagnostics

Client: **Hadassah Mother and Child Center**
Design Firm: **Creative Services Department**
Designers: **Robert Pearlman, Hong Chow**

THE HADASSAH MOTHER AND CHILD CENTER

Client: **Private Exercise**
Design Firm: **Evenson Design Group**
Designer: **Ken Loh**

Client: **Keynote Arts Associates**
Design Firm: **VR Design**
Designers: **Victor Rodriguez, Stan Capshaw**

Client: **US West—Making Music Together**
Design Firm: **Vaughn Wedeen Creative, Inc.**
Designer: **Steve Wedeen**

MAKING MUSIC
TOGETHER

Client: **Chamber of Commerce, Eugene, OR**
Design Firm: **Funk and Associates**
Designer: **Sandy Lui**

Client: **Opti World—Eagle Eye golf sunglasses**
Design Firm: **BHA/Bergeron Hamel**
Designers: **Michel Bergeron, Matthew Taylor**

Client: **TenderCare Veterinary Medical Center**
Design Firm: **Rassman Design**
Designers: **John Rassman, Amy Rassman**

Client: **Innovative Golf Products**
Design Firm: **Primary Design, Inc.**
Designer: **Christine Hardiman**

Client: **Crown Equipment Corporation**
Design Firm: **Graphica**
Designers: **Mark Stockstill, Nick Stamas**

Client: **The Corporation for Cultural Literacy**
Design Firm: **Jon Wells Associates**
Designer: **Jon Wells**

Client: **Elkhorn Construction, Inc.**
Design Firm: **Carter Design, Inc.**
Designers: **Jim Carter, Heidi Domagala, Kendra Murphy**

Client: **The Oregon Arena Corp.—Rose Garden**
Design Firm: **Runk and Associates**
Designer: **Tim Jordan**

Client: **University Hospital of Cleveland**
 International Summit
Design Firm: **Herip Design Associates, Inc.**
Designers: **John R. Menter, Walter M. Herip**

Client: **Great Additions and Renovations**
Design Firm: **PLD**
Designers: **Lisa Busch, Chris Adams**

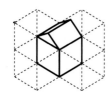

Client: **Allen & Pierce Securities**
Design Firm: **Cullinane Design, Inc.**
Designer: **Lucinda Wei**

Client: **Bill Graham Presents**
 San Francisco New Year's Eve Party
Design Firm: **Clement Mok Designs**
Designers: **Andrew Cawrse, Mark Crumpacker**

Client: **Sahara Hotel & Casino**
Design Firm: **Concept Marketing Design**
Designers: **Reg Avey, Sam Marguccio**

Client: **DAM Creative**
Design Firm: **DAM Creative**
Designer: **Dana A. Meek**

Client: **Washington Adventist Hospital**
 Physicians Campaign
Design Firm: **Alphawave Designs**
Designer: **Douglas Dunbebin**

Client: **Little Mountain Woodworks**
Design Firm: **Prime West, Inc.**
Designer: **Tom Culbertson**

282

Client: **Kraft Foods—Island Mountain Kona**
Design Firm: **Muts & Joy & Design**
Designer: **Katherine Hames**

Client: **Jones Murphy, Inc.**
Design Firm: **Visually Speaking, Ltd.**
Designer: **Craig P. Kirby**

Client: **Peninsula Naturopathic Clinic, P.S.**
Design Firm: **The Print Source, Inc.**
Designer: **Theresa L. Ramsdell**

Client: **Jewish Healthcare Foundation of Pittsburgh**
Design Firm: **Bradley Brown Design Group, Inc.**
Designer: **Robert Kiernan**

Client: **Centerior Energy**
Design Firm: **In-House**
Designer: **Jeffrey P. Wilhelm**

Client: **Bread for the City & Zacchaeus Free Clinic**
Design Firm: **Levine + Associates**
Designer: **Mike Myers**

Client: **Tucson Community Food Bank**
Design Firm: **Boelts Brothers Associates**
Designers: **Eric Boelts, Jackson Boelts, Kerry Stratford**

Client: **Urban Harvest**
Design Firm: **CROXSON Design**
Designers: **Stephen Croxson, Michael Ratcliff**

283

Client: **Enviprotech**
Design Firm: **Mifsud Design**
Designer: **William Mifsud**

ENVIPROTECH

Client: **S.D. Johnson—Orca**
Design Firm: **Mires Design, Inc.**
Designer: **John Ball**

Client: **California Fig Advisory Board**
Design Firm: **The Kellett Group**

Client: **Caffé Diva—Fine Coffee**
Design Firm: **Funk and Associates**
Designers: **Beverly Soasey, Sandy Lui**

CAFFÈ DIVA

Client: **Moonlight Mushrooms**
Design Firm: **A to Z Communications, Inc.**
Designers: **Alan C. Boarts, Kathy Kendra**

Client: **Hunter Unlimited**
Design Firm: **Bloch + Coulter Design Group**
Designers: **Victoria Coulter, Thomas Bloch**

Client: **Wayside Waifs**
Design Firm: **Muller + Co.**
Designer: **Jon Simonsen**

Wayside Waifs

Client: **East Africa Safari Co., Ltd.**
Design Firm: **Metamorphia**
Designer: **David Ludwig**

Client: **Joan Simmons**
Design Firm: **Agarwal Graphic Design**
Designers: **Joan Simmons, Prashant Agarwal**

Client: **Concepts Nouveau**
Design Firm: **DAM Creative**
Designer: **Dana A. Meek**

Client: **Sinomex**
Design Firm: **Kelston**
Designer: **Michael Stinson**

Client: **UGC Consulting**
Design Firm: **Rassman Design**
Designer: **John Rassman**

Client: **Phoenix Partnership**
Design Firm: **Webster Design Associates**
Designer: **Dave Webster**

Client: **Dairy Farmers, Inc.**
Design Firm: **Corporate Design Associates**
Designer: **Matt Taylor**

Client: **Workhorse Design, Inc.**
Design Firm: **Workhorse Design, Inc.**
Designers: **Constance Kovar, Anthony Taibi**

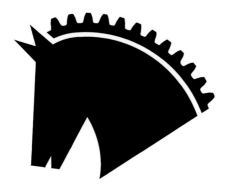

Client: **Titleist—golf club division**
Design Firm: **Laura Coe Design Associates**
Designers: **Ryoichi Yotsumoto, Lauren Bruhn, Laura Greer**

Client: **MDL Information Systems, Inc.**
Design Firm: **Steve Naegele Design**
Designer: **Steve Naegele**

Client: **Horizon Healthcare**
Design Firm: **Vaughn Wedeen Creative, Inc.**
Designer: **Dan Flynn**

Client: **The New England Patriots**
Design Firm: **Evenson Design Group**
Designer: **Ken Loh**

Client: **Jitters**
Design Firm: **Insight**
Designers: **Tracy Holdeman, Sherrie Holdeman**

Client: **Long Island Fund for Women & Girls**
Design Firm: **Fleury Design**
Designer: **Ellen Fleury**

Client: **Magical Theatre Company**
Design Firm: **Minx Design**
Designer: **Cecilia Sveda**

Client: **The Cleveland Indians**
  1995 American League Champions
Design Firm: **Herip Design Associates, Inc.**
Designer: **John R. Menter, Walter M. Herip**

Client: **Love Box Company—3 on 3 Basketball Tournament**
Design Firm: **Love Packaging Group**
Designer: **Tracy Holdeman**

286

Client: **Gerry Zack Fine Art Photography**
Design Firm: **Alphawave Designs**
Designer: **Douglas Dunbebin**

Client: **Score America**
Design Firm: **Laura Coe Design Associates**
Designers: **Ryoichi Yotsumoto, Laura Coe Wright**

Client: **The American Child Foundation**
Design Firm: **Evenson Design Group**
Designer: **Glenn Sakamoto**

Client: **Child Guidance Center of Dallas**
Design Firm: **Peterson & Company**
Designer: **Nhan Pham**

Client: **Brooks Howard**
Design Firm: **Evenson Design Group**
Designer: **Glenn Sakamoto**

Client: **Brookhaven Business Division**
Design Firm: **R.M. Design/Illustration**
Designer: **Rock Morris**

Client: **Larry's Shoes**
Design Firm: **Blanchard Schaefer Advertising**
Designer: **Mari Madison**

Client: **Tres Hermanas Restaurante**
Design Firm: **Funk and Associates**
Designers: **Beverly Soasey, Tim Jordan**

287

Client: **The Design Foundry**
Design Firm: **The Design Foundry**
Designers: **Tom Jenkins, Jane Jenkins**

Client: **Die Works**
Design Firm: **Webster Design Associates**
Designer: **Andrey Nagorny**

Client: **Berkano Productions**
Design Firm: **Berkano Productions**

Client: **Radio Gabby**
Design Firm: **Evenson Design Group**
Designer: **Glenn Sakamoto**

Client: **Rock and Roll Hall of Fame + Museum**
Design Firm: **Nesnadny + Schwartz**
Designers: **Mark Schwartz, Joyce Nesnadny**

Client: **All Brite Laundry**
Design Firm: **Y Design**
Designer: **Clement Yip**

Client: **Integral Training Systems**
Design Firm: **Halleck Design Group**
Designer: **Ellen Rudy**

Client: **Senior Sports Classic VI**
Design Firm: **Boelts Brothers Associates**
Designers: **Eric Boelts, Jackson Boelts, Kerry Stratford**

Client: **Minneapolis Institute of Arts**
Design Firm: **Rapp Collins Communications**
Designer: **Bruce Edwards**

Client: **MODA—1950's-inspired furniture**
Design Firm: **Zust & Company**
Designer: **Mark Zust**

Client: **Square D**
Design Firm: **Graphica**
Designer: **Drew Cronenwett**

Client: **Lab for Interactive Future**
Design Firm: **Coleman Design Group**
Designers: **John Coleman, Amanda Grupe**

Client: **Fatigue Busters**
Design Firm: **Dever Designs, Inc.**
Designer: **Jeffrey L. Dever**

Client: **International Planning, Inc.**
Design Firm: **Magic Pencil Studios**
Designer: **Scott Feldmann**

Client: **Rubbermaid**
Design Firm: **BHA/Bergeron Hamel**
Designers: **Michel Bergeron, Ross Charters**

Client: **Alimenterics, Inc.**
Design Firm: **Frank D'Astolfo Design**
Designer: **Frank D'Astolfo**

289

Client: **The Seattle Foundation**
Design Firm: **Hansen Design Company**
Designer: **Pat Hansen**

Client: **International Trade Service Corporation**
Design Firm: **Herip Design Associates, Inc.**
Designers: **Walter M. Herip, John R. Menter**

Client: **Aultman Hospital**
Design Firm: **Liggett-Stashower**
Designer: **Ed Kagy**

Client: **Akili**
Design Firm: **Graphic Concepts Group**
Designer: **Brian Wilburn**

Client: **Best Press**
Design Firm: **Sullivan Perkins**
Designer: **Brett Baridon**

Client: **Corbis**
Design Firm: **Hornall Anderson Design Works, Inc.**
Designers: **Jack Anderson, John Anicker, David Bates**

Client: **4-M Plumbing and Heating**
Design Firm: **Edward Howard & Co.**
Designer: **Mark Grieves**

Client: **Tsunami Dive Gear**
Design Firm: **Mires Design, Inc.**
Designer: **John Ball**

Client: **Harbinger Corporation**
Design Firm: **Rousso + Associates**
Designer: **Steve Rousso**

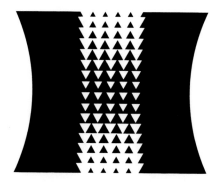

Client: **Haynes and Boone**
Design Firm: **Phinney/Bischoff Design House**
Designer: **Dean Hart**

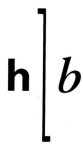

Client: **Hoffman Estates Chamber of Commerce**
Design Firm: **Identity Center**
Designers: **Wayne Kosterman, Darin Hasley**

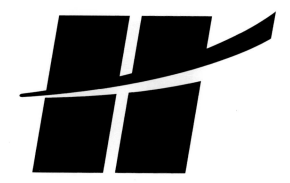

Client: **J. Gilberts**
Design Firm: **Muller + Company**
Designer: **David Shultz**

Client: **Nancy L. Held—photographer**
Design Firm: **Joseph Dieter Visual Communications**
Designer: **Joseph M. Dieter, Jr.**

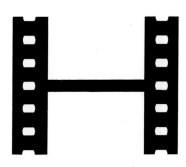

Client: **Italian Hotel Reservation Center**
Design Firm: **Julia Tam Design**
Designer: **Julia Chong TAm**

Client: **American Heart Association—Arizona Affiliate**
Design Firm: **SHR Perceptual Management**
Designers: **Karin Burklein Arnold, Nancy Ogami**

Client: **J. Sadler Company Home Improvement Specialist**
Design Firm: **Harrisberger Creative**
Designer: **Lynn Harrisberger**

291

Client: **Prime Group Corporation**
Design Firm: **Shubz Graphics**
Designer: **Jeff Shubzda**

Client: **Pacific Cascade Federal Credit Union**
Design Firm: **Funk and Associates**
Designers: **Kathleen Heinz, Tim Jordan, Diane Fowler**

Client: **Primetek**
Design Firm: **The Visual Group**
Designers: **Ark Stein, William Mifsud**

Client: **XactData Corporation**
Design Firm: **Hornall Anderson Design Works, Inc.**
Designers: **Jack Anderson, Lisa Cerveny, Jana Wilson, Julie Keenan**

Client: **Southern California Gas Company**
Design Firm: **Julia Tam Design**
Designer: **Julia Chong TAm**

Client: **Patricia Franklyn International**
Design Firm: **Identity Center**
Designer: **Wayne Kosterman**

Client: **Robert Reichert—photographer**
Design Firm: **Katherine Machado Design**
Designer: **Katherine Machado**

Client: **Sattelite Studio
   computerized graphics/design firm**
Design Firm: **Sattelite Studio**
Designer: **Shahen Zarookian**

Client: **John Milly**
Design Firm: **John Milly Designs**
Designer: **John Milly**

John Milly Designs

Client: **Gatx—Quest for the Best**
Design Firm: **Corporate Design Associates**
Designer: **Matt Taylor**

Client: **Thompson Engineering**
Design Firm: **Rousso + Associates**
Designer: **Steve Rousso**

Thompson

Client: **Votation**
Design Firm: **Levine + Associates, Inc.**
Designer: **Mike Myers**

VOTATION

Client: **Quick Quality Press**
Design Firm: **JCnB Design**
Designer: **Jane Nass Barnidge**

Client: **Quantum Commercial**
Design Firm: **Z•D Studios, Inc.**
Designers: **Mark Schmitz, Cherie Peltier**

QUANTUM
COMMERCIAL

Client: **Glass Apple Theatre**
Design Firm: **Graphica**
Designer: **Al Hidalgo**

Client: **Weidenback Construction**
Design Firm: **Milkboy Design**
Designer: **Michael White**

293

Client: **Hot Stuff, Inc.**
Design Firm: **Wild Garlic Art Studio**
Designer: **Zbigniew Jastrzebski**

Client: **ACA Joe**
Design Firm: **AERIAL**
Designer: **Tracy Moon**

Client: **Bod-E**
Design Firm: **Mires Design, Inc.**
Designer: **Mike Brower**

Client: **The Cleveland Indians—Indians Team Shop**
Design Firm: **Herip Design Associates, Inc.**
Designers: **Walter M. Herip, John R. Menter,
    Duane L. Dickson**

Client: **Conceptual Litho Reproductions**
Design Firm: **Edward Walter Design, Inc.**
Designers: **Edward Walter, Rodrigo Benadon Oks**

Client: **Clarus Corporation**
Design Firm: **Parsons & Maxson, Inc.**
Designer: **Cathy Gerken**

Client: **Matthews Media Group, Inc./N.E. Place**
Design Firm: **Alphawave Designs**
Designer: **Douglas Dunbebin**

Client: **Hudson Bar and Books, Ltd.**
Design Firm: **Tom Fowler, Inc.**
Designer: **Thomas G. Fowler**

Client: **Schwener Electric**
Design Firm: **Schwener Design Group**
Designers: **Diane Schwener, Cynthia Brown**

Client: **Michael Grasso—Lightfall**
Design Firm: **Pat Davis Design**
Designer: **Andrea Johnston**

Client: **Eagle River Winery**
Design Firm: **Rassman Design**
Designer: **John Rassman**

Client: **Witherbee Wilderness Camp**
Design Firm: **The Weller Institute for the Cure of Design, Inc.**
Designer: **Don Weller**

Client: **LA Gear—Light Gear**
Design Firm: **Mires Design, Inc.**
Designer: **Scott Mires**

Client: **The Upper Deck Co.**
Design Firm: **Mires Design, Inc.**
Designer: **José Serrano**

Client: **South American Exchange, Ltd.**
Design Firm: **DeMartino Design, Inc.**
Designer: **Erick DeMartino**

Client: **Sugar Loaf Creations**
DBA American Coin Merchandising
Design Firm: **Pollman Marketing Arts, Inc.**
Designer: **Jennifer Pollman**

Client: **M.G. Swing Company**
Design Firm: **Mires Design, Inc.**
Designer: **Mike Brower**

Client: **Village Paper Company**
Design Firm: **Kurt Roscoe Design**
Designer: **Kurt R. Roscoe**

Client: **Image Gate**
Design Firm: **Z•D Studios, Inc.**
Designers: **Mark Schmitz, Chris Maddox**

Client: **Cazenovia Public Library**
Design Firm: **Jowaisas Design**
Designer: **Elizabeth Jowaisas**

Client: **28 State**
Design Firm: **Larry Miller Productions**
　　　　　　 Communication Via Design
Designer: **Victoria Adjami**

Client: **Royal Executive Dining**
Design Firm: **Roger Christian & Company**
Designer: **Roger Christian**

Client: **Coffee Factory**
Design Firm: **AXIOMA, Inc.**
Designer: **José Bila Rodriguez**

Client: **Fabrique**
Design Firm: **Pure**
Designer: **James Pettus**

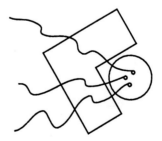

296

Client: **Excellon Automation**
Design Firm: **Perlman Company**
Designer: **Bob Perlman**

Client: **Auburn Arts Commission**
Design Firm: **Art O Mat Design**
Designers: **Jacki McCarthy, Mark Kaufman**

Client: **Greater Pittsburgh Convention &**
Visitors Bureau, Inc.
Design Firm: **Elias/Savion Advertising**
Designer: **Ronnie Savion**

Client: **Centennial Lakes Dental Group**
Design Firm: **Ikola designs...**
Designer: **Gale William Ikola**

Client: **College of ACES, University of Illinois**
Design Firm: **Information Services**
Designers: **Myung Lee, Ann Bergeron, Michele Plante**

Client: **DC Comics/Batman**
Design Firm: **The Sloan Group**
Designers: **Wyndy Wilder, Chris Mogen**

Client: **The Kilgannon Group**
Design Firm: **Rousso + Associates**
Designer: **Steve Rousso**

Client: **United Mortgage**
Design Firm: **OMNI Studio**
Designers: **Claudia Hon, Jeff Rashid**

Client: **WGMS 103.5—Classical Radio Station**
Design Firm: **Sullivan Perkins**
Designer: **Christman Fifer**

297

Client

299

300

Designers

302

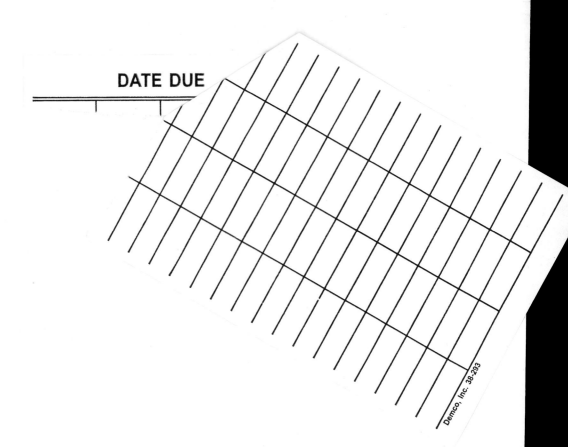